Boyd Webb

Boyd Webb

Jenny Harper

AUCKLAND
ART
GALLERY

TOI O TĀMAKI

Published in association with Museums Aotearoa

First published in 1997 by
Auckland Art Gallery Toi o Tāmaki
PO Box 5449, Auckland 1, New Zealand

In association with Museums Aotearoa
PO Box 10928, Wellington, New Zealand

All photographs reproduced courtesy
Boyd Webb and remain his copyright

Copyright © Auckland Art Gallery Toi o Tāmaki
Jenny Harper, Lynne Cooke, Ian Christie,
Ron Brownson, Boyd Webb

ISBN 0 86463 218 5 (hardback)
ISBN 0 86463 219 3 (paperback)

Editor: Christina Barton, Wellington
Design: David Faulls, ExPress Communications, Auckland
Book project management: Michael Till, Wellington
Printed in Hong Kong through David Ling Publishing, Auckland

Published on the occasion of the exhibition BOYD WEBB
Auckland Art Gallery Toi o Tāmaki, 28 November 1997 – 22 February 1998

Contents

Preface

This book is a testament to the complex, remarkable and poignant imagination of Boyd Webb. Although he has not lived in New Zealand since 1972, I am convinced that his formative years here inflected his vision. He was introduced to contemporary sculpture and conceptual art while at the Canterbury University Department of Fine Arts in Christchurch, and his work there obviously formed the basis of his subsequent practice. Likewise, he relates the muted tones of some of his early work to the grey-greens of the New Zealand bush, while the vivid colours of his more recent work have a clarity which may reflect the piercing nature of light in New Zealand. But he also revelled in London, a city at the centre of the art world. Like Frances Hodgkins and Len Lye, his forebears from this country, he was nurtured and developed further by the varied opportunities provided in the northern hemisphere.

Boyd Webb offers an opportunity to review and assess the photographs and films which form the bulk of his practice through the 25 years since his departure. Three interpretative essays present a variety of art historical, imaginative and theoretical frameworks within which to consider Webb's work, and an interview with the artist offers further unique insights into his imagination. These texts newly reveal Webb's long-standing interest in the theoretical and practical apparatuses of science and his desire to meld this interest with the intuitive and creative field of art. It is telling that the authors of these texts are based in Wellington, New York and London, for they reflect the international nature of Webb's practice and recognise his crucial place in the field of contemporary art.

Both John Leuthart, executive director of Museums Aotearoa, and I join in thanking Jenny Harper, associate professor of art history at Victoria University of Wellington, for co-ordinating the publication and selecting the accompanying exhibition. We are proud to be associated with the work of Boyd Webb and we join her in wholeheartedly acknowledging and thanking everyone who made it possible.

Chris Saines
Director
Auckland Art Gallery

Acknowledgments

This publication emanates from New Zealand, the country of Boyd Webb's birth; it is a recognition of his achievements and the esteem in which he is held here. Putting it together involved the efforts of many people and I should like to acknowledge and thank them. John Leuthart, executive director of Museums Aotearoa, has been responsible for overseeing the fruition of an idea which has lurked in many guises for at least a decade. He has been a driving force behind the publication and all aspects of the overall project. Chris Saines, Director of the Auckland Art Gallery, readily embraced the proposal with his great enthusiasm and quickly agreed that his gallery should publish the book. I am grateful to them both.

I am very grateful too for the contributions of the other writers: Lynne Cooke, curator at New York's Dia Centre, and Ian Christie, a film historian from London. In addition, Ron Brownson, senior curator at the Auckland Art Gallery, interviewed the artist during a recent trip to New Zealand, enabling his eloquence to appear in written as well as visual form. It was wonderful throughout to work with writers with such professional commitment.

I am particularly grateful to Ron Brownson also for his great support at particular moments, including the use of his legendary eye when it came to the layout of images. David Faulls designed the book, adroitly organising text, scanning transparencies and overseeing its production with an enviable calm. Michael Till provided expertise and encouragement at a critical early moment and stayed on to see the publication through.

To my colleagues in the art history department at Victoria University of Wellington, I owe a considerable debt. Phillipa Hayden, David Maskill and Damian Skinner all shouldered extra work this year and provided moral support; and Tina Barton edited all the texts, but in particular my section, with unusual skill. It is rare to find a colleague with such unflinching intellectual generosity – and the ability to see what was meant in initial drafts. I would also like to thank Victoria University reference librarian, Barbro Harris, for her help with bibliographic details.

Boyd Webb is represented by several galleries in London, New York, Auckland and elsewhere. Thanks are due to various individuals in these: Sue Crockford in Auckland has been wonderfully enthusiastic and supportive from the beginning; Antonio Homen and Jason Ysenburg from the Sonnabend Gallery in New York were helpful when I visited New York in 1996; and there has been a continuous stream of useful information from staff at the Anthony d'Offay Gallery in London, in particular, Robin Vousden, Simon Lee, Margot Heller and Stefania Bortolami.

Families and friends are important sources of information and support and I should like to thank Derek Webb, Neil Dawson, Gretchen Albrecht, Jamie Ross and Christine Hellyar, all of whom readily shared reminiscences. Thanks are due to Christopher and Judy in Auckland who gave me space to work when I was there; and also to Sarah, who learned to look after herself at weekends during the course of this project.

This book has been published on the occasion of an exhibition which will tour New Zealand and then further afield from November 1997 when it opens at the Auckland Art Gallery. While it has been conceived as a monograph, rather than an exhibition catalogue, it does not stand entirely alone and there are many people who have supported the development and realisation of the exhibition, whom it is important to acknowledge. The exhibition touring agency of Museums Aotearoa have organised the national and subsequent international tour of the exhibition. As well as John Leuthart, thanks are due to Stacey Neale, Donna Campbell and Tony Cairns at Museum Directors' Federation.

The British Council contributed to the exhibition development as part of its 1997 Link programme. In particular, Paul Smith and Barbara Procter have been enthusiastic and supportive from the beginning. The exhibition and publication have both been generously supported by Creative New Zealand as part of the realisation of their arts development and presentation objectives; in particular, I would like to thank their visual arts programme adviser, Gregory Burke. I should like to thank Colenso, Auckland, for supporting the creative development of the exhibition's promotion. Lastly, the extensive tour of the exhibition in this country could not have proceeded without the financial support of the Chartwell Trust – to Rob Gardiner grateful thanks from all of us for his continuing championing of artistic creativity.

No art exhibition or publication is possible without the artist. Boyd Webb not only made the extraordinary work which this book celebrates, but he cared about every detail of this publication and the exhibition. It has been both memorable and a huge privilege to work with him – I readily acknowledge my admiration for him and his work.

Jenny Harper
Victoria University of Wellington
September 1997

Middle of the road sculpture
1971

Unruly truths

The work of Boyd Webb

Jenny Harper

Serendipitous and questioning, puzzling and perverse, Boyd Webb's photographs move stealthily between illusory construction and two-dimensional fact. They draw on the techniques of scenography and model-making, the strategies of staging and display, to create a compressed universe in which human and animal, object and image, set and scenario are made, positioned, captured and dissected. His work is paradigmatic of our current moment in its provocative scrutiny of the codes of vision and narrative – he manipulates both to pose questions about meaning and reality, to test old truths and propose new laws.

My task in this essay is to trace Boyd Webb's developing practice, establishing his roots in New Zealand in the 1960s, and the progress of his career since 1972 in England; and to give an account of his work which establishes its artistic and conceptual context. Always fascinated in his looking and galvanised by his imaginings, Webb has an eye for the particularities of his situation and the possibilities to which it gives rise. He has moved from conceptual sculptural practice to photographing theatrical tableaux for their own sake, from constructing cosmological expanses and making ecological statements to intimating bodily interiors with the sparest of means. Despite quite radical changes in his work, however, consistent threads of interest are discernible throughout.

Boyd Webb was born in Christchurch, New Zealand, in a country which was rural in character, a former colony emerging as a distinctive nation state. He trained in sculpture at the Canterbury University Department of Fine Arts, which in the late 1960s was beginning to feel the effects of the profound challenges radical art practices were posing to the conventional teaching and making of art. Webb was exposed to a range of new ideas and an opening of the field to embrace carving, construction and the use of re-cycled material, as well as the incorporation of film, music and theatre. Under the impact of Tom Taylor, Canterbury had become an environment where discussion and experiment were actively encouraged.

This became possible due to the influence of minimal, post-minimal and conceptual art which dramatically shifted the emphasis of art-making from object to situation and from product to process. Knowledge of these current practices began to filter into the art school through the pages of *Studio International* and *Artforum*. They were explored by Boyd Webb, as well as by fellow students such as Pauline Rhodes and Neil Dawson.

As early as 1971, Webb's work was cannily re-directing the examples of Richard Long and Carl Andre to rather deflationary and certainly locally-oriented ends. Thus in **Middle of the road sculpture** **1971** (facing), he squeezed shaving cream onto the tarmac of a quiet Christchurch road to create what was at once a credible centre line, a 'floor-piece' of ephemeral foam, and some markings which had the consistency and colour of New Zealand's favourite meringue, the pavlova. What remains – the photograph and the title – locates it as an early example of conceptual art in this country and a prototype of what Webb's work was to become. Not only does it document an ephemeral act, operating in the space between image and fact, but it also shows the artist ruffling the surface of suburban normality, making us wonder what the absent residents of that safe place would have made of this art student with his shaving cream can in the middle of their street.

Webb's student work was full of neo-dada, post-Duchampian playfulness. With characteristic irreverence he tested the boundaries between art and life to re-enact scenarios which effectively shift our perspective, drawing attention to the overlooked, forcing us to confront everyday situations anew. He was fascinated by the construction and detection of differing levels at this time, exploring these in large outdoor works and documenting them photographically. In one, he half buried large-scale, unfurled flags which somehow still appear to fly; in another, he re-created a tidal shoreline of flotsam and jetsam threading itself along the undulating grassy knolls surrounding the car park of the Department of Fine Arts (tarmac doubled as sea), inducing an uncertainty about the realistic jetty he built for the piece.

Eels
1971

While some of his works did exist as three-dimensional sculptures, others were made to be documented like *Middle of the road sculpture.* These included works like *Eels* **1971** (opposite), in which pre-frozen eels masquerade as the fence around a suburban garden behind an angelic child fishing in the Avon river, bringing something atavistic and vaguely repulsive into Christchurch's genteel centre. Or in a number of untitled works where Webb placed ordinary objects in natural locations according to resemblances they established with what should or might be already there: 'sprouting' ballpoint pens in a mangrove swamp; rubber suction caps on some seaside rocks; eels on a railway track. Alternately, he made serial images which established a kind of narrative or progression in time, like *Tennis match*, a series of twelve photographs and captions which were an episodic presentation of a subterranean game of tennis watched by a half-visible, but attentive umpire. This frame-by-frame work recalls Keith Arnatt's performance, *Self burial* **1969**, in which he sequentially documented in nine photographs his disappearance underground. Both artists use photography to re-situate sculpture in time and both works ironically render their subjects invisible, inventing metaphors for the end-game gambits of conceptual art at the time.

Like Arnatt, Webb also incorporated performance into his work, but unlike his British (and New Zealand) peers, he never appeared in the work himself. With his absence, Webb positioned himself as the 'master'-mind of each scene.

His final vanishing act established the *modus operandi* of his work to come. This was his end of year submission for his degree at Canterbury where he made his examiners attend a performance from which he would ultimately demur, leaving in his place a secretary who made an appointment for them to view his submitted work – at a later date. By requiring his examiners to go through the motions of gaining access to his work, he had in fact turned them into performers and, therefore, elements of the work. What better signal of the ways in which he would use actors and friends in shaping his subsequent work?

Webb's student work was dematerialised to the point it could fit in a file in a drawer. Finally submitting it in a leather briefcase, he hinted that he was ready to leave.[1] His mission, as it turned out, was to continue his studies at the Royal College of Art in London, a destination several of the more promising students from Ilam had already reached.

London was an obvious place to go for a New Zealander at this time. Not only was England still regarded by many as 'home', but London itself was a lively centre for contemporary art, a scene marked by an irreverent attitude to the past and a breakdown of the traditional distinctions between high and popular culture. If British pop artists like Richard Hamilton and David Hockney had chosen to look to the world of mass consumer culture for their subject-matter, their iconoclasm was re-inforced by challenges to the authority and value of art with the emergence of performance, process and conceptual art in the 1970s.

Webb became familiar with the work of artists like Stuart Brisley,[2] Richard Long, Hamish Fulton, Stephen Willets, and another New Zealander living in London, Bill Culbert. Such artists sought to work outside the conventional contexts of art, seeking out new subjects and using new materials, and often undertaking one-off site-specific work in the studios of SPACE, the ambitious, artist-run warehouse in a derelict area of St Katherine's Docks which was to become a symbol for the alternative ideologies promulgated at the time.[3]

Webb was not alone in choosing the Royal College of Art for his postgraduate studies.

Already a number of promising young New Zealanders had studied there, from painting students like Bill Culbert, John Drawbridge, Don Peebles, and Pat Hanly, to fellow sculptors and proto-conceptualists, like Stephen Furlonger, John Panting, Billy Apple (then Barrie Bates) and Darcy Lange. The Royal College at this time was known as a school which was producing interesting artists – recent graduates and concurrent students included Richard Wentworth, Tony Cragg, Alison Wilding, Richard Deacon and Brian Catling. Webb enrolled as a sculpture student, producing little at first, but taking the opportunity to find his way around London.

Webb's work at the College was pretension-pricking and incisive in character. His pieces suggested fragmentary and seemingly absurd narratives; they were directed to reveal unusual aspects of the human character or to re-enact his particular brand of pseudo-scientific investigation. From his new situation in England, he was well placed to make material which anatomised his observations of the mores and behaviour of both British and New Zealand cultures.

Webb's first public performance six months after his arrival in London was full of irony and affectionate nostalgia for New Zealand. Staged in New Zealand House in the Haymarket as part of the opening of 'Six New Zealand artists',[4] Webb's entire contribution was designed to bring aspects of Kiwi life into the heart of London.

The performance was a social event which ran parallel to the preview. Webb reconstructed in microcosm a 1950s dance at a small town hall, just like that in any part of rural New Zealand. He arranged for two or three couples dressed in party clothes to dance cheek-to-cheek beneath streamers in a sectioned-off area of the ballroom. While the band played foxtrot tunes, beer, potato chips, and the ubiquitous lamingtons and meringue cakes were served.

Unlike that of his fellow artists, all of Webb's work for the show referred to his country of origin. His three photographic pieces drew on plainly New Zealand subject matter: a deadpan re-presentation of several pages from a training manual for dental nurses, a series of sepia-tinted photographs of the famous shearer Godfrey Bowen at work, and a piece which related to a particular Maori myth associated with a famous lake in the South Island, *Wakatipu* **1973** (p 68).

Lake Wakatipu, the subject of a well-known painting by 19th century landscape artist, Eugène von Guérard,[5] and a favoured scenic destination for tourists seeking the unspoilt beauty for which New Zealand is famous, was not simply described but rendered in duplicate. In his version, Webb paired black and white photographs of the lake and surrounding hills with images of his own knees sticking out of a bath; toes parallel trees on the lake's shore and limbs mimic the pitch of the mountain slopes. He sought to illustrate the Maori legend which had it that the mountains around that lake were formed by the knees of Te Tipua, a fearsome monster; and that the mysteriously rising water levels of this inland lake were attributable to the mythic monster's deep breathing. It was this which he wanted to illustrate by using his own body in the bath and a caption which read: 'Breathe in... breathe out... breathe in...' The accompanying text which related the legend assured his readers that no (scientific) explanation of the phenomenon had ever been offered, although it had been investigated by the Royal Society.

It is interesting to note the aspects of this work which were to re-emerge and develop as Webb matured. Not only does he re-configure 'reality' into a model derived from the human

SCRIPT FOR "PREVIEW"

Boyd Webb 1974

VENUE   The preview of the Six New Zealand Artists exhibition at the Auckland City Art Gallery in August 1974.

ACTION   When the preview is well underway, two men arrive, one short and the other tall. (They have invitations.) The tall man is blind i.e. he wears dark glasses but has no other distinguishing features. The short man leads him slowly around the show describing and explaining the work to him, encouraging him to touch the three dimensional work. They partake of drinks etc. and may converse with other people if spoken to, in fact behave in keeping with the occasion. After an hour or so when they estimate that most people have seen them, they change the dark glasses over and repeat the performance, the tall man leading the short and now blind man around and explaining the work to him. The second circuit should take as long as the first and when completed they quietly leave.

NOTES   *1 The actors must be unknown i.e. not acquainted with the Auckland or New Zealand 'art scene'. If professional actors are used they should be reasonably un-exposed.*

    2 There must be a marked difference in the actors' heights.

    3 The actors should be attired appropriately i.e. dark lounge suits or similar.

    4 Secrecy concerning the arrangements etc. must be maintained up to and during the performance if the piece is to be successful.

body and a few everyday props, but he creates a scenario which serves as a demonstration of both a principle of western science (Archimedes' law of displacement) and simultaneously as a visualisation of a physical fact for which – as in myth – there can be no logical explanation. Reason is both referred to and undermined. Webb's use of his own body via the medium of photography was typical of a variety of conceptual strategies employed by artists at this time. His cataloguing of what might be called 'found' sculptural situations in everyday New Zealand life in this and other work in the exhibition was not lost on British reviewers of the show.[6]

For the New Zealand version of 'Six New Zealand artists', Webb included entirely different work, choosing to reverse his London strategy and show only performance and photography-based pieces 'made in England'. All from 1974, the nine works included **Holothurians** (p 58), **The tenant at no 51**, **The sheep carcass**, and **Locating the water table prior to the seasonal re-positioning of the Plimsoll line**, each heavily reliant on text for its meaning. As well as rendering his ideas episodically, Webb revealed his continuing fascination with making art which engages with the laws of science. He also continued to tease his audience with works which refused to take themselves seriously, where humans role-play so that attention is drawn to the situation at hand. This is true of **Preview**, the opening night performance, which though admittedly a more covert piece than its London counterpart, went virtually unremarked by the less sophisticated New Zealand audience.[7]

The instructions for Webb's Auckland performance are recorded in **Script for preview 1974** (previous page). Two people of distinctly different heights – if actors, 'reasonably unexposed' – were to arrive at the exhibition's opening together, taking turns at playing a part. At first the taller of the two had to don a pair of dark glasses to suggest that he is blind. Half way through the evening the spectacles were exchanged and their roles unobtrusively swapped. In Auckland, a number of guests were mystified as these rather formally dressed men walked around the exhibition, the one vigorously describing the work on display to the other until their departure, which went as unannounced as their arrival. Some commented; others pretended not to notice. For many there was simply a tinge of oddity about the event.[8]

Webb's invention of characters who play out certain roles or display bizarre behaviour was typical of his Royal College of Art work. For example, *Herbert Groves* **1973** (p 69) is an amateur lichenologist, who has cultivated lichen in his mouth. The scenario Webb constructs for him is equally as disorienting as a blind man in an exhibition – for Groves is a compulsive gambler who frequents the betting office in order for his lichen to grow. The fungus needs the algae and their symbiotic relationship needs the fuggy atmospheric conditions typically generated by the tension of betting for high stakes; just as their host is dependent on placing the next bet. Not only is Webb drawing attention to the drives and diversions of a welfare-dependent class, but typically he is constructing a scenario in which a biological cycle is mirrored in everyday life – and vice versa.

Like Eugene Ionesco or Samuel Beckett, Webb exposes the details of natural life and the psychology of the human mind in terms of the absurd. As with these dramatists, text and image work within the closed universe of theatrical space. Images function like theatre stills, moments of arrested action which encapsulate his strangely instructive scenarios. Webb remains in the role of director but, as the 1970s proceeds, his instructions become more laconic as he relies less on text. In *Mrs Barnes* **1976** (p 71), for instance, two disjunctive and unexplained images are framed together. They unsettle because they use the conventions of drama to worry the line between reality and fiction, and because the 'truthfulness' of photography is deployed to test whether the viewer will be taken in by the scene: has the baby fallen from the pram, or is it mere pretence?

London and its environs provide the backdrop for several such quirky and telling scenarios. However, Webb ventured into the countryside also: to hang a maggot-infested sheep carcass over a river a few weeks prior to fishing there, or to record a nervously fidgeting tramp orchestrating the business of his dog in a lane in *Altruism and the law of diminishing returns* **1976** (below). As usual, we are left pondering the image. Has the tramp managed the event to gain the sympathy of the young woman who inadvertently soils her shoe? What will he gain in return for his altruistic act? Absurd as this interaction might be, it nonetheless points

Altruism and the law of
diminishing returns
1976

to a larger transaction, operating as a metaphor for society at large; for this street-wise tramp orchestrates a ruse from which he benefits, by meeting an artificially-created demand.

The dramas which take place on the railway track, outside the betting office, in lanes and fields, indicate Webb's detailed observation of human behaviour. Intrigued as he is with the human will to make something work against the odds, he chooses to comment on society by focusing on individuals. However weird or macabre their actions, he records their foibles with acumen and sympathy.

Webb was beginning to make a mark in London. The Robert Self Gallery in Covent Garden exhibited his Master's degree portfolio in a group show in 1975, organised his first solo exhibition in 1976, and published the catalogue, *Tableaux*, in 1978. That year also, his work was shown in Düsseldorf and Athens, as well as further afield in England. Later in 1978 the Whitechapel Art Gallery organised the first of two important exhibitions of his work.[9] And in 1981 Webb first exhibited at the Anthony d'Offay Gallery in London. He has shown there ever since.

It is indicative of his growing reputation that Gilbert and George, who also showed at the Robert Self Gallery and then at Anthony d'Offay's, commissioned Webb to make their portrait in 1977. *The microbe as Van Leewenhoek may have seen it* (pp 72-73) is a rare instance of Webb using recognisable subjects in his photographs, though here the 'living sculptures' were posed to perform in a typical Webb scenario. For they adopt the role of scientists, observing and recording a microscopic organism in a work which recalls Webb's fascination with science, and the ongoing absorption with the dialectics of vision and knowledge which informs much of his subsequent work. By choosing to depict his fellow artists in a scenario which describes something we cannot ordinarily see, he reminds us of the disjunction between perception and cognition which the project of technological advancement has been designed to redress.

Webb brought to the London art scene his sense of the absurd, his powers of intelligent social observation, honed as an outsider in a new situation, and an increasing commitment to photography as the ultimate form his sculptural practice would take. When, in the late 1970s, Webb began working almost entirely inside his East London studio, a new phase of his work began.

Instead of staging his scenes in real locations, he began utilising a limited number of props, creating each scene from scratch, becoming more conventionally sculptural. He constructed sets out of found and purchased materials and worked on the staging of his photographs to the point where each embodied the rituals of its making. With their makeshift, do-it-yourself quality, his sets had a certain prosaic charm which may be associated with his New Zealand roots. Certainly he seemed to prefer an air of 1950s tattiness, which he now fabricated rather than found in real situations.

Having at first revelled in the environs of the city of London, he is now retreating from his urban milieu and creating his own universe within his large studio. His work became entirely self-sufficient as, ingeniously, he let ordinary items serve multiple and unusual purposes from the prosaic to the grandiose. Linoleum variously denoted landscape elements or sky; hardboard the side of a ship; the same piece of ghastly green carpet became a planetary surface in *Supplicant* **1984** (p 89), and a feeding ground for a few blackbirds in *Sphagnum* **1985** (p 98);

and stiff painted paper in *Glorious morning* **1986** (p 104) was made to suggest new planetary beginnings. Webb explored the visual, textural and physical qualities of wire-wool in several works made in 1987 – using it to flow like water (though horizontally) from a tap, to fix a cello against a violet backdrop in *Coda* (p 110); to denote a stricken plane with smoke trailing from it in *Untitled* (p 115), and to become a nest for coconuts atop a cosmic form, with blackened bananas in *Rudiments* (p 109), while egg yolks, toast, a circular saw blade and even a rat feature in related versions of this work.[10]

Webb inserted real people into many of these fabricated sets to act as human subjects in his artificial but strangely familiar worlds. He chose his models from among friends and colleagues, but also selected unknown candidates from the local neighbourhood and persuaded them to take part in his dramatic tableaux. As with the *Preview* performance in Auckland, he preferred protagonists without defining characteristics, their anonymity allowing them to more fully represent or symbolise a wider humanity.

His models are posed to be photographed. They interact with a range of everyday props – knitting needles, toasters, telephones, globes. In a somewhat strange reversal, the real objects

One bird
1981

of his three-dimensional tableaux are treated as impermanent transient forms, whereas the permanent tangible product is the elusive two-dimensional photographic image. But as the 1980s proceed, the register of artifice is turned up a notch as he moves away from creating believable spaces, simple interiors like museum dioramas, stage sets, or the interior of a photographer's studio, to construct ever more ambiguous spaces – oceans, subterranean realms, intergalactic zones. At the same time, the scale of his photographs increases so that by their dimensions and physical qualities they increasingly assert a tangible presence.

Although from time to time Webb exhibited installations, sculptural pieces, and made films, still photography was his primary *métier* from now on. However, his photographic practice remains closely related to – an instance of – current sculptural and conceptual strategies. Photography functions as documentation of work *in situ*, the residue which remains in the aftermath of a serendipitous bringing together of found and fabricated materials. Thus his work is akin to that of fellow sculptors, Bill Woodrow, Tony Cragg and Richard Wentworth, who make sculpture from scavenged and re-cycled objects. Such a practice has its forebears in the tradition of Marcel Duchamp, but also in the dada photomontages of Hannah Höch, Raoul Hausmann and John Heartfield and the constructions of Kurt Schwitters.

In addition, Webb's staged tableaux owe a debt to the highly formalised and rigid conventions of classical Greek tragedy and the ritualised set pieces of traditional Noh and Kabuki theatre. Here, individuals are mobilised as representatives of humanity, posed in order to comment on our perplexing and at times perverse relation to the world.

But if a lineage and a context can be established for Webb's work in the arenas and history of high art, we must also look for its sources in the realm of popular culture. As Webb himself describes it, his work is 'a series of lame but colourful cartoons combining the concerns of the Victorian genre painter and the techniques of a mail-order catalogue photographer'.[11] His scenes are brightly lit and highly representational. Their startling naturalism belies their extra-ordinary content. Like the Victorian set pieces to which he refers, we are led to believe that Webb sees himself playing, at one end of the spectrum, the role of moral commentator and, at the other, the chronicler of social farce. And like the commercial photographer, his increasingly gorgeous blow-ups seduce with their slick surfaces and their loving depiction of the wasted remains, the residue of the 'toil and commerce of industrial urbanised society'.[12]

For almost a decade, then, Webb worked with this limited range of props to construct artificial worlds in which his often isolated characters struggle to make sense of things, to overcome the obstacles he so frustratingly places in their way. While the nature of their ordeal may seem prosaic, it tends to provoke the viewer to ponder the larger questions of our human condition – leading inevitably to our seeing his work as aspiring to the condition of myth. Thus in *The light and shade of expedience* 1979 (p 75), simply changing a light bulb becomes an exercise in co-operation, a metaphor for hope and renewal, and a pun on the politics of inter-racial exchange. *The light and shade of expedience* alludes also to those dialectical oppositions which permeate western language and thought structures, as well as the many awful jokes commonly made at the expense of various professional, trade and racial groups.

Identification and categorisation based on physical differences are also alluded to in *The mandatory second opinion* 1978 (p 76). Here Webb draws on a Sufi tale of two blind men feeling a different part of the same elephant and simultaneously describing a different beast to

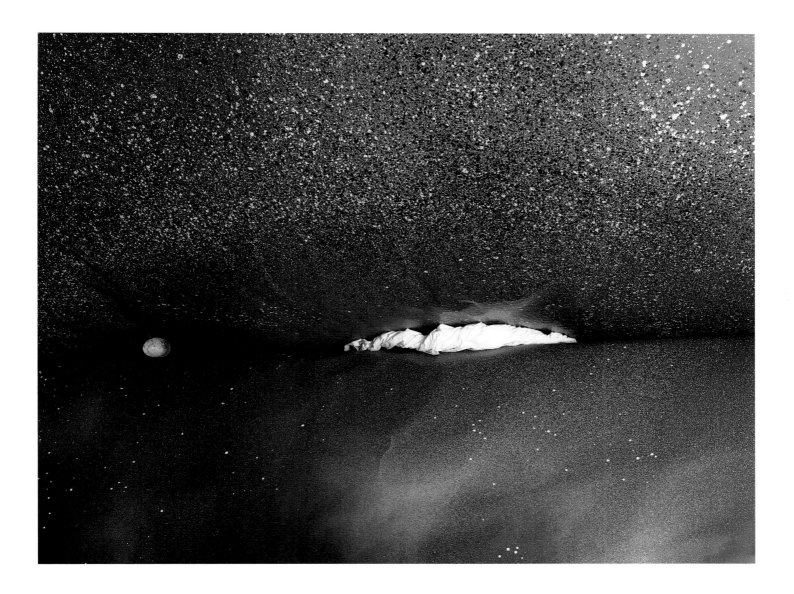

each other, to enigmatically suggest that the testimony of experts cannot always be relied on if they endeavour to classify without comparing like with like. This game of mix and match seems oddly futile, especially when it is set in a sterile 'office' and when the rubbish bin is clearly the ultimate fate of the object of study.

As the 1980s proceed, humour gives way to pathos as Webb's vision becomes rather more bleak. Environmental concerns emerge as the world we know appears to be threatened. Now the artificiality of the materials he uses has a double edge, as 'nature' becomes fabricated and patently fake. Survival has become an issue. In ***One bird* 1981** (p 19), eggs, bird and rock are isolated, the only remnants of a blasted, if still evocative, world. In ***Guillemots* 1981** (p 166) the drama of the human condition is condensed into a buffeted, bedraggled and lonely figure, his shirt soiled with guano as he protects a number of eggs in a felt hat. But there is ambiguity here, for we are not sure if he is stealing the eggs (and getting soiled in the act), or endeavouring to save the species. Is he a bird lover, or someone who understands the economic value of the waste material with which he is splattered?

Clenched
1985

An air of catastrophe hangs over Webb's work. He shows us human frailty and isolation, the transience of things, a world beleaguered by forces beyond control – natural cataclysm, acts of war, the machinations of a retributive god. In *Abyssogramme* **1983** (p 86) and *Dry-eyed* **1984**, we are witnesses to the aftermath of such events. Wreckage lies at the bottom of the ocean, or bobs forlornly in a sea of green carpet. Impassive and silent, this world continues to exist but now without human intervention or control. No wonder, then, that old telephones float hopelessly, reduced to a futile conversation between themselves; that encyclopediae lie inane and abandoned in an undersea zone; and that birds fly 'dry-eyed' over the scene of a shipwreck.

Webb proposes that such disasters may also be wreaked by the destructive action of an uncaring deity, conceived in works like *Autostrafe with handicap* **1983** (p 88), *Nemesis* **1983** (p 87), *Tortoise* **1984** (p 91) and *Tosser* **1985** (p 101), as a semi-naked man, whose actions are scarcely more meaningful than the games children play. The consequences of his actions are for the viewer to perceive and question. Why can't the man playing with his inflated toy planes see that if their cargo of bombs is dropped, they will destroy not only the camouflaged camp, but also his own foot poking through the soil? How long can he hold onto his pile of loaves before they are unleashed on the dinosaurs quietly grazing the grass beneath? Doesn't that man realise the damage he is causing as he pitches little globes at the perched coconut orbiting on a vulnerable planet? We are all too aware of the effects of exhalation as the slightly corpulent agent of vengeance in *Nemesis* blows into a tube inflating a balloon which destroys a house on the earth's surface; and it is we who become implicated in our desire to intercede.

Webb tests the logic and meaningfulness of the supposed connection between action and reaction, cause and effect. But his pessimistic vision is tempered as well by instances where there is reason for hope. In *Nourish* **1984** (p 95) *Salvage* **1984** (p 84), and *Replenish* **1984** (p 90), we see not gods but men (and children), who find succour and support in this desperate universe. In *Salvage* a child rescues another from a paper sea, while a third clambers onto a jetty, and in *Lung* **1983** (p 51), a man in a boat holds fast to his companion turning an accordion into an 'organ' of hope. There is a great tenderness here too, where humans are shown as both reliant on each other and needful of support. Webb places them within the natural order – a man suckles a whale, greenery is used as bedding for a child – and also in the familiar comforts of home, with toast and fruit loaf, telephones and musical accompaniment.

Ironically, the poignancy of these images is effected through their artifice: unseen forces are operated by no more than strings; a battered stool holds up a 'deity'; planets are as thin as coloured paper; the earth may be mere textured carpet. Webb reinforces the artificial hold we have on the real by these means, at the same time allowing privileged access to more than the senses normally perceive. For he both exploits the potential of photography and transcends it. Webb uses the camera to transcribe what is real in all its tangible specificity, enabling him to create scenarios which, although staged, are made of things we know and recognise. He allows us – as all good dramatists do – to extrapolate from the specific to the meta-physical where much of the meaning of his work lies. He poses things so that we see both above and below, inside and outside, and – from the outer reaches of space – back and through from one realm to another. We are led to suspect the thinness of the tissue which contains our physical lives and to become aware of the magnitude of what lies beyond.

Mortise
1988

From now on, however, Webb moves away from using real people in his work, tending to concentrate on making the materials he uses suggest his concerns more obliquely. In works like *Coppice* **1986** (p 105) and *Cupid's sting* **1986** (p 103), patterned and coloured papers are arranged in overlapping and intersecting layers, which unsettle as, at one and the same time, they concede their superficial quality and assert the vastness of an unfolding space. Skilled at simulating the macro-cosmic and the infinitesimal concurrently, Webb alludes to new beginnings in both works: the cosmological courtship in *Cupid's sting* and the meticulous arboreal grafting procedure in *Coppice.*

In a new series begun in 1988 after *Santa Ana,* an installation made in Los Angeles,[13] Webb suggests a more precise level of connection to environmental issues. Drawing inspiration from science and the literature of science,[14] Webb gives inflatable (but often deflated) plastic animals a central role in his universe. These works operate as a mournful eulogy for the world, the surface of which has become increasingly synthetic. In this slick new world, technological innovation is mirrored by an increasing tendency towards abstraction and, in almost perverse contradistinction, an ever greater fascination for the careful delineation of shiny artifice. Objects and animals multiply here not through the processes of natural birth and propagation, but through the actions of genetic manipulation – through cloning and mass production and, in images like *Two views* **1988** (p 124), they are doubled through mirroring and reflection.

This is a distinctly antediluvian world, one in which the organic and manufactured float, hover or are veiled in a soupy fluid of an eerily elegiac hue. In *Denizen* **1989** (p 53), for example, a Portuguese man o' war floats on the surface of a polythene ocean, its inky dye flowing over its transparent body and into the sea from which its tendrils gain sustenance. This allusion to chemical warfare is reinforced in *Plant* **1989** (p 121), where flattened ducks are arranged around a sheet of model parts for a toy military vehicle; and its sepulchral tone echoed in *Croup* **1989** (p 123), where choked ducks are displayed like trophy heads in an 'atmosphere' suggestive of polluted skies in the northern hemisphere.

Even the more strongly registered colours of *Undrained* **1988** (p 118) and *Beleaguer* **1989** (p 120) present an apocalyptic vision of the world as it might become; the helplessly askew tigers and the vivid reds and yellows of sunset positing an end to our tyranny. As in his works from the early 1980s, Boyd Webb is continuing an exploration of the clash of nature and technology and, as before also, his particular synthesis of fact and fiction into a vaguely subversive allegory encourages the conclusion that the sterile seas and stranded animals may be the result of our (in)action.

But there is a point to global politics and, although Webb remains a reluctant interventionist (assuming the role of prophet rather than activist), he also takes a positive stance at times, seeming to suggest that the interdependence and mutuality of animal and human can itself be beneficial. In *Chattels* **1989** (p 126), for instance, our attention is drawn to a herd of giraffes valiantly ferrying the small globe which appears to be our only hope; and in *Suckling,* a diptych of 1989 (pp 128-129), twins inside each of two jellyfish apparently setting off in opposite directions nevertheless leave room for the anticipation of renewal as we ponder the enjoining of human and marine life. This is perhaps a re-working of the myth of Romulus and Remus, the abandoned Roman twins suckled by a she-wolf, one of the myths on which western civilisation was founded. It is as if Webb seeks an updated version to ensure the sustenance of

human life. Strangely, too, the evocative beauty of the 'wild' life he uses is not entirely lost, for these plastic toys have their own fragile grace despite their lifelessness.

With Webb's speculations on the world, the universe, and this era of ecological imperilment, it is not surprising that images of generation and re-generation began to appear more substantially than before. Latterly his interest has turned to imagining and fabricating the workings of the human body and fathoming how, in turn, the processes of the body can operate as a metaphor for life. Since 1993 he has indulged an abiding interest in human biology. Fertility and the interior workings of the body have become his primary subject matter.[15]

A series of photographs made for the Indian Triennale[16] in 1994 in which he explores his obsession with biology, exposing for our consideration the potency and poignancy of sex and generation, indicates this new direction. Here the artistic progenitors of Webb's new work may be found in the biomorphism and sexually-charged works of surrealists like Max Ernst who made a Sadean universe out of erotic materials, and the painted tidal fantasies of Yves Tanguy.

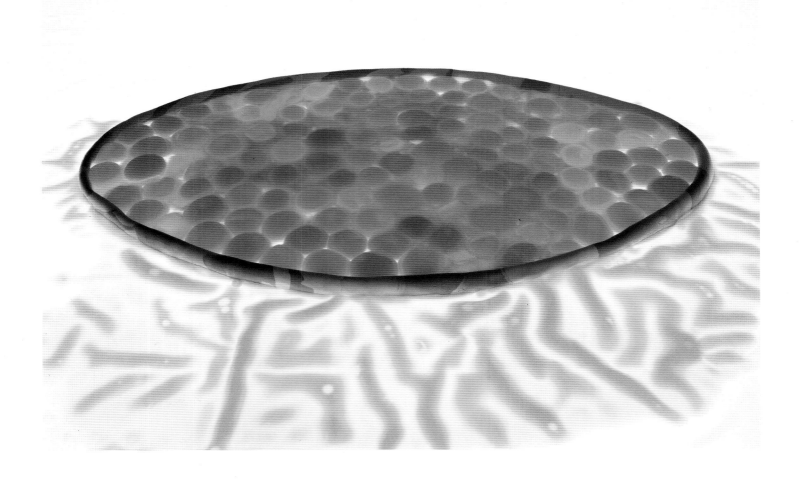

Shoal
1994

Like these surrealists, Webb consistently probes some of the most pervasive anxieties of our time; we become aware of the vaguely subversive nature of his preoccupations, disporting themselves in these revelatory vignettes.

This is not the first time Webb's work has been sexually loaded. Earlier works such as ***Replenish* 1984**, ***Cupid's sting* 1986**, and ***Moth* 1989** (pp 90, 102-103, 122), for example, all in some sense recall the dis-ease which can be traced back to his earliest work like ***Eels* 1971** (p 12). But the new pieces like ***Donor* 1994** and ***Ebb* 1993** (pp 142, 143), which speak of the hubris of fertility and generation, of the coming on and wasting of potential, are especially disquieting in this era of assisted reproduction and safe sex. Another biological struggle is laid out in ***Tutelar* 1993** (p 140), a sporting scene in which the inertness of sepulchral plasticine signifies the most motile of human organisms swarming towards an egg yolk. A fragmentary and marginal human appearance suggests our partial role in the larger drama of existence. We have become accustomed to Webb's work presenting us with a puzzle, to grappling with the teleology of his world view as we look. Are we witnessing an early moment in a comedy or tragedy of reproduction? Are the sperm going to reach their goal? Is the manually-proffered egg being given or withheld?

Webb has become interested in overtly representing the magic and repulsion of the everyday. Rather than making the more lofty statements of the 'cultivated' individual, he dissects mundane bodily functions and places what is rarely exposed or discussed on display. Swirls of bloodied urine unashamedly issue from a latex penis in *Sob* **1993** (p 132); and there is no dispute about the turd-like, phallic and disgusting appearance of *Stool* **1994** (p 137) – both images transfix with their power simultaneously to appal and intrigue. Other works allude to the mechanics and detritus of sex or suggest gender power plays, as in the menacing vulvae arranged around fragmentary and malformed sperm in *Parole* **1994** (p 25). But whatever he exposes to our view, Webb's representations of the messiness and vicissitudes of nature are transfigured as images of exquisite elegance.

Zygote **1993** (p 136), a transformation of ordinary spittle and twisted grey clay, introduces the final group of Webb's works I will discuss in this essay. It is one of a group in which art and biology meld as his working method becomes increasingly aligned to his personal scientific interest. Here photography is used neither to describe actual space nor as the final proof of the veracity of perspectivalism, but rather as an exposition on light and matter.

In *Zygote* the elemental, molecular and biological are transfixed in a remarkable rainbow of colours achieved by capturing the effects of materials transfigured through the imposition of light. And in *Nonage* **1995** (p 152-153), Webb invokes scientific photography and microscopy in a cloying clinical embrace to show foetal shapes being nurtured in the safety of a laboratory, as in *Shoal* **1994** (facing), where egg yolks double as a captivating experimental site.

Now, in the 1990s, Webb conveys not only the minuscule but the galactic not as a painted surface – like the clumsy fabrications of the museum diorama – but as a numinous realm, a suspension of materials in substance which in turn is illuminated by light. Thus if we compare *Tract* **1996** (pp 150-151) with *Clenched* **1985** (p 21), we are not looking at a folding surface a little distant from the camera lens, but instead we have become aware of light emanating in a less distinguishable space which functions more as a volume. Webb's newly sub-liminal vision of a biology which registers as a luscious yet viscous surface is suspended here. In works like *Agar and celeste* **1996** (pp 160-161) and *Aurora with serum* **1996** (over), barely legible vestiges of life mingle and multiply.

Rather than studying complicated diagrams and analysing the conventional scientific description of what interests him, Webb prefers to imagine how a particular form or process might be and then to fabricate his own version.[17] He uses light to expose surfaces which suggest what lies immediately behind observable reality, representing this in the harsh glare of bright studio lighting to ensure that the colours remain 'wasabi-like' in their strength.[18]

Curiously, at this juncture in our technological history, Webb eschews the new digital image-making possibilities many of his contemporaries are embracing. Rather than manipulating his images on computer,[19] Webb continues to labour over the careful preparation of materials, the lighting of his set-ups, and finally the camera's action. He manages to achieve the most discombobulating effects by making simple ingredients (tinfoil, dust, wall paper paste and plastic) take on the eerie sheen and synthetic hues of digitally-produced objects.

Webb is not seeking to articulate an entirely simulated universe, but rather to retain the co-ordinates of the real to postulate the realms of the unseen and finally to construct the imagined. For he continues to believe in that adage which is hoary with age but perhaps still

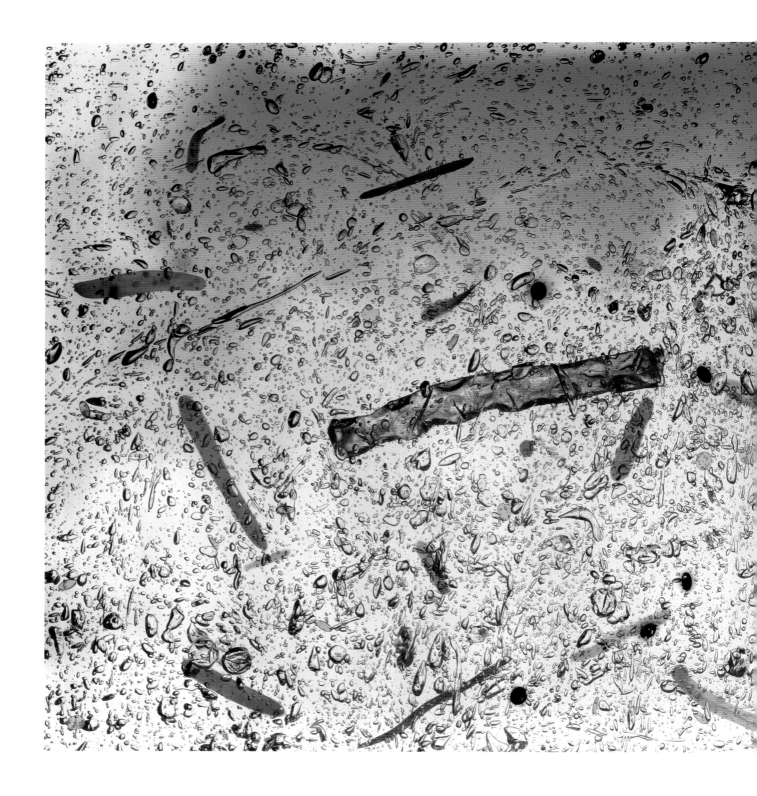

true, that one can see the whole universe in a grain of sand. Ironically, given the nature, scale and sophistication of his photographic practice, Webb embraces his medium, not as many postmodern practitioners have – to expose the conventional and constructed nature of vision – but to recall photography's originary function: to capture and describe the real, even though he increasingly witnesses it retreating.

Webb has consciously explored a variety of strategies to engage the viewer with his work. Earlier exterior scenes were set up and documented as if they were real, but their reality was undermined by misleading juxtapositions and disjunctive texts and titles. Subsequently, his

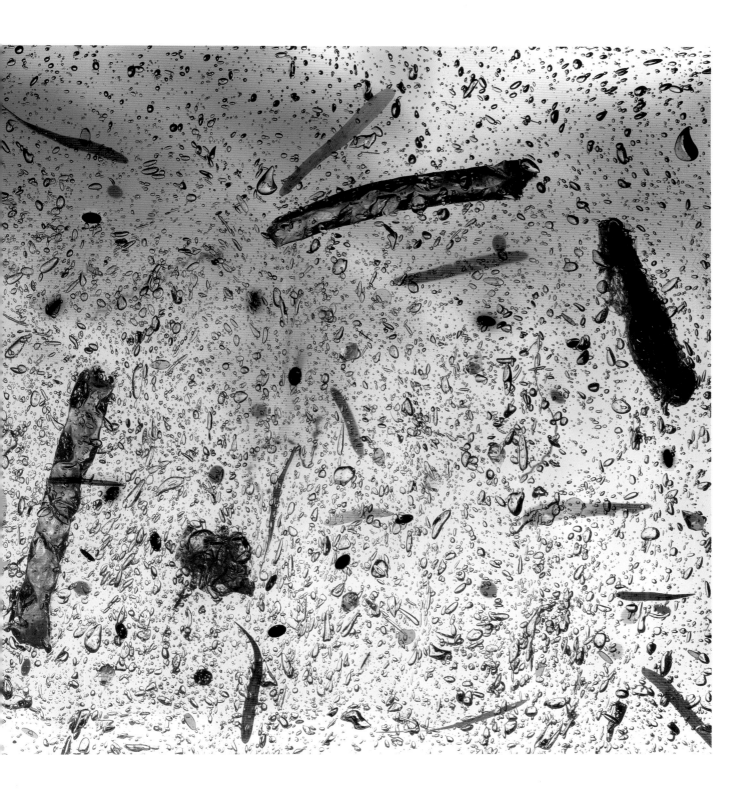

Aurora with serum
1996

spaces became dramas set within credible space into which we cautiously stepped, aware that each image was purposefully framed for our consumption. During the 1980s, he fabricated the sites of his ecological and cosmological dramas, fetishising the props he used, and inviting us to observe these from a more proximate place, as if looking down at a map. Now, he brings the lens far closer, holding up slices of life for our dissection.[20]

He has shifted from showing us the scientist looking into the microscope as he did in ***The microbe as Van Leewenhoek may have seen it*** (pp 72-73) to allow us to occupy that role. Such intimacy brings his perspective ever nearer, though the artifice is never in doubt. There is nothing homogenous about the rhetoric of his vision; and nothing simple about the self-consciousness with which he compels us to look.

Boyd Webb's works offer a shifting perspective between reality and illusion, surface and depth. They function as visual propositions about the processes of life. And, as photographs, they engage in the discourses of vision and representation enabling a profound meditation on the ability of art to replicate life. For as viewers, we are left

> shimmer[ing] between wondering at (the marvels of nature) and wondering whether any of this could possibly be true.[21]

Notes

1 The thesis submission was presented in a folder contrived to look like a British passport, with this and other pieces being placed in an embossed leather briefcase which opens like a book. While the passport may allude to his intention to travel for further study, the briefcase was intended as a pun about the succinct nature of his output to date. Interestingly, Webb's 'life's work' can still be contained within a briefcase.

2 Webb vividly recalls seeing a Brisley performance at a house owned by the Goethe Institut in Queensgate soon after his arrival in London – its programme was particularly rigorous and cutting-edge. In this case, the artist submerged himself in a bath of pigs' entrails for a full day with only his nostrils exposed, making a statement about the material mess of life, in addition to vindicating behaviour standardly excluded from the realm of art.

3 SPACE (Space Provision, Artistic, Cultural and Educational) was initiated by Bridget Riley and Peter Sedgley, who managed to persuade the Greater London Council to lease 60,000 square feet of warehouse space for a peppercorn rental prior to its re-development into a marina.

4 'Six New Zealand artists' was initiated by Merwyn Norrish, the newly-appointed acting High Commissioner to London, who was keen to have New Zealand presented abroad as more than the producer of butter and rugby players. He approached a director of the Felicity Samuel Gallery, New Zealander Antoinette Godkin, and asked her to arrange an exhibition of contemporary art. All six exhibiting artists had received scholarships to attend the Royal College; the other five were John Panting, Darcy Lange, Ken Griffiths, Stephen Furlonger and Terry Powell. Subsequently, Godkin was invited by the Queen Elizabeth II Arts Council of New Zealand to organise a national tour of this show under their auspices – it opened at the Auckland Art Gallery in August 1974.

5 Eugène von Guérard's *Lake Wakatipu with Mount Earnslaw, Middle Island, New Zealand* 1877-79, is in the collection of the Auckland Art Gallery.

6 For example, Richard Cork wrote that Webb's work indicated a close knowledge of the international vanguard. In particular, he commented on the sculptural qualities of Webb's series of sepia-tinted photographs of sheep shearing which were in the exhibition: 'Although his decision to photograph the various stages of a sheep-shearing session in sepia tints may seem, superficially, to be the act of an innocent country lad, it really springs from a sophisticated understanding of how other modern artists have studied similar rituals in the same stage-by-stage manner. Absorbed in his superbly practised task, the shearer drives his razor through the wool like a sculptor shaping his raw material, and Webb emphasises this analogy by presenting the whole operation as a series of decisive moments which gradually transform the animal's whole identity' (*Evening Standard* 16 Feb 1973). 'Six New Zealand artists' attracted considerable publicity despite showing for only one week. As well as Cork's review, others appeared in: *The Financial Times*, 17 Feb (Vaizey, M. 'Six from New Zealand'); *The Sunday Times*, 18 Feb (Russell, J. 'A sense of place'); *The Times*, 20 Feb (Brett, G. 'New Zealanders leave their legends behind'); and *The Times Diary*, undated [1973] (PHS. 'Life is not all butter and rugby').

7   The Auckland performance was noted by only one reviewer, Geoff Chapple in 'Seeing Eyes for Six', *New Zealand Listener*, 28 September 1974. Very few, if any, would have been aware of the English duo, Gilbert and George, despite their **Singing sculpture 1969** having been brought to Melbourne and Sydney by John Kaldor in 1973. This performance involved swapping a walking stick and glove as each took a turn at switching the tape recorder to replay the theme song, 'Underneath the arches'.

8   Note, for example, the letter of C. Alexander McCleod to the *Auckland Star*, whose primary purpose was to berate the Queen Elizabeth II Arts Council for bringing such poor quality work to New Zealand and 'expensively toting [it] around the country'. He finished his outburst by informing readers that, 'The only viewer who seemed happy was a totally blind man who was enjoying the comments of his friend and guide' (Letters to the editor, 26 August 1974).

9   The second was in 1987. *Boyd Webb*, an exhibition catalogue, was published on this occasion with an essay by Stuart Morgan, 'Global strategy'.

10   See the Whitechapel, 1987, exhibition catalogue cover, the invitation to the 1987 exhibition at Galeria Cómicos in Portugal, and the page work in *Artforum*, ('Inanimations', April 1987, pp 112-113) as well as **Rudiments** and **Schism 1987**.

11   Morgan, Stuart, in London: Robert Self Gallery, 1978. *Tableaux.* unpaginated.

12   Bennett, David, 1989. 'Art and rubbish'. *Art and Text*. Autumn, pp 98-105.

13   Webb was short-listed for the Turner prize for his installation, **Santa Ana 1988**, an installation commissioned by MoCA, Los Angeles. Erected within the museum, a giant bespoke breathing marquee became the size of a zeppelin when inflated but was reminiscent of malnourished ribs when deflated. Viewers looked into it through face-sized holes, surprised to see another's face in a suspended mirror. Disembodied countenances waxed and waned in intensity as the tent breathed, its wheezing recalling Santa Ana, a dry winter wind which originates in the desert, clearing the city of haze – later to be returned by the sea breeze.

14   Sources range from the generalised impact of contemporary photographs of outer space (for example, in *Space images*, Lustrum Press, 1982) to direct quotation from an historical source as in **Aurora and aspic 1988** (p 116) showing two steel engravings from the nineteenth century publication *Wood's Natural History* (G.F. Routledge).

15   What Webb said of two large murals commissioned by Channel 4 in London summarises his concerns at the time: 'They are songs from the age of bio-technology, a fibre-optic view of a world where biological tissue and ingredients of the human psyche – desire and lust, hope and despair, are mated' (Channel 4 press release, 15 November 1994).

16   The exhibition 'Boyd Webb' was organised by the British Council as Britain's contribution to the Indian Triennale. It toured extensively through India, after Webb won the main prize at the Triennale, and a larger version concurrently toured in Britain.

17   For example, although the abdominal tract may have provided a beginning point for **Tract 1996** (pp 150-151) the completed work intimates far more: the vastness of galactic space and the intimacy of a petri dish. The interior becomes interchangeable with the exterior as if, at the time, the artist had one eye to a microscope and the other to a telescope.

18   A vivid term, used by Webb in conversation, 20 July 1997.

19   The one exception to date is the digitally manipulated popcorn in **Asteroid and kidney stone** (pp 62-63) made for the Hayward Gallery's 1996 exhibition, 'Spellbound'.

20   Literally, in fact, since Webb has recently created a number of scenarios (**Retort 1996**, pp 156-157, and **Passage 1996**) within narrow aquaria-like spaces, inserting transparent substances such as hair-gel and pieces of other material into these, to be closely observed.

21   As Lawrence Weschler suggests of visitors to the Museum of Jurassic Technology in Western Los Angeles, a museum with something of a cult following in the contemporary art world, in *Harper's magazine*. 'Inhaling the spore, field trip to a museum of natural (un)history'. September 1994, pp 47-58.

Eclipse
1982

Motives for metaphor

Boyd Webb and film

Ian Christie

Desiring the exhilarations of changes:
The motive for metaphor, shrinking from
The weight of primary noon,
The ABC of being.
— Wallace Stevens, *The Motive for metaphor*

A forgotten piece of popcorn beneath a cinema seat, against all odds, succeeds in germinating, nourished by a diet of coffee dregs and flickering light reflected from the screen. Then, wedged by chance in a passing boot sole and carried to another theatre, it finds a mate. Boyd Webb's animated film *Love story* resulted from an invitation to contribute to a group exhibition celebrating the centenary of cinema in 1996.[1] It was perhaps a rare case of Webb being provided with a subject, or at least a theme, and the opportunity to realise this collaboratively.

It wasn't however the first time that this most cinematic of artists has worked with film. Twice before, at roughly ten year intervals, Webb has moved beyond his accustomed role as *metteur en scène* of witty and disturbing tableaux to make moving-image works. Somewhat in the tradition of the 'historic' avant-garde, like Léger's, Duchamp's and Dali's films in the 1920s, it is as if Webb has wanted to take stock of his current interests, and to see what working in film as an amateur can offer by way of summary and contrast.[2] Since so much of his photographic work looks like frozen moments from unimaginable movies, the effect of actual movement is disconcerting.

In fact Webb's first moving-image work, *Guard film* 1973, made while he was studying at the Royal College of Art, played directly on the paradox of using film to represent stasis, and on film's unreal 'reality effect'. A ceremonial guardsman stands unmoving at his post, then abruptly marches ten yards to the left and back, repeating this manoeuvre three times. Made as a film loop and shown life-size on a special curved screen, this was in many ways typical of the 'expanded cinema' work being created by a number of London artist-filmmakers in the 1970s.[3] Less typical, perhaps, though entirely characteristic of Webb, is the deadpan humour. A recent arrival in London from New Zealand, he adopts a banal tourist subject like a picture postcard 'made strange'.

Film, and the newly accessible medium of video, were attracting many young artists at this time, and London was a centre of this cross-fertilisation. The London Filmmakers' Co-op was launched in 1966 and had become a focus for the screening and subsequent distribution of American, German and British work. The London art schools were also open to a lively overlap of film and performance, often under the nominal heading of sculpture. Webb's contemporaries at the Royal College of Art in 1972-5 included a number of future independent film-makers, such as Phil Mulloy, Keith Griffiths, and the Quay Brothers. In 1974 he scripted a video piece, *Holothurians* (p 58), which catches exactly (and gently mocks) the self-referential climate of this period, summed up in the title of the first major London retrospective, 'Film as film', in 1979.[4] In Webb's script, a man writing at a table and with a pen that runs dry is rhymed with the image of a sea cucumber filled with 'ink'. In this Magritte-like scene, the subject is writing or dreaming itself – the precursor of a recurrent Webb motif.

As photographic prints became Webb's main medium and his reputation grew, these early moving-image pieces might have remained marginal, symptomatic of the mixed media London scene in this period. But the two more substantial films he has since undertaken suggest a wholly different relationship to his better known work. Whether we consider them extensions or summaries, they are undoubtedly integral – and, once seen, they inescapably condition our view of Webb's 'stills'.

To understand how *Scenes and songs* and *Love story* resonate, it is worth sketching several contexts of production and interpretation. I will propose three: first, the reflexive art documentary movement in Britain in the 1970s and 1980s; second, the relationship between animation and the surrealist tradition; and finally, Len Lye considered as a counterpoint to Boyd Webb.

If we commonly think of art documentaries as worthy, didactic displays of received wisdom, this may be a reaction to the mediocre examples that used to be a staple in art cinema programmes, serving to differentiate these from the normal run of movies. However, films about living artists have often prompted sophisticated collaboration and technical innovation – such as Henri Storck's *Le monde de Paul Delvaux* 1946, Cluzot's *Le mystère Picasso* 1956 and Jack Hazan's mimetic portrait of David Hockney, *A bigger splash* 1974. The first sign of a new collaborative approach in British art documentaries was James Scott's *Richard Hamilton* 1969, made with the active involvement of the artist to accompany an exhibition. Scott (who is the son of the painter William Scott) went on to explore new ways of closing – or posing – the gap between gallery art and film in a series of inventive works, from *The great ice cream robbery* to *Chance, history, art.*[5]

Encouraged by Scott's and other examples, the Film Department of the Arts Council of Great Britain began in the mid-1970s to commission increasingly ambitious works, in which film-makers were encouraged not only to collaborate with living artists, but to develop quasi-fictional approaches to the art of the past, and also to reflect such activities as photography, improvised music, performance and community art – all new concerns for the custodians of state patronage.[6] Not since the mid-1930s, when artists inspired by surrealism and constructivism first infiltrated the Post Office information film unit, had the staid genre of British documentary become such a focus for innovation.

It was in this climate that Webb created *Scenes and songs from Boyd Webb* for the Arts Council in 1984, working with the director Philip Haas, who had previously collaborated on a film with the 'living sculptures' Gilbert and George.[7] Ostensibly *Scenes and songs* consists of a series of Webb's cosmic and mythic tableaux from this period filmed as performances, with varying degrees of movement and action. Three little boys clamber over a landscape, like pantomime castaways, jumping and fighting, their antics observed by a periscope that cruises a painted sea. A woman swings in a celestial cradle, amid giant, orbiting vegetables; a man rolling a cigarette has his crotch burnt by a circling toy jeep that bears a cradle aloft; rabbits produce eggs; and a fish-woman tries to melt a block of butter under water.

The prevailing tone is mock-heroic: if these are in some sense gods or figures from legend, they are represented by actors who are only too human, in settings that flaunt their artifice and economy. Like one of the radical new opera productions then current[8] – an association reinforced by the film's 'songs', a series of parodic *lieder* – Webb's microcosms from this period disdain bombast and deploy sly humour seemingly to invoke the mythical and the magical for a sceptical age.[9] Yet the film also does something more: it takes us behind and between the scenes.

The first image we see is of a street, with a group of children peering through a window into the studio; and the first tableau includes the cruising periscope which will later be capped

Salvage
1984

with a yoghurt pot. Between the tableaux, Webb himself appears three or four times, emerging from a shop with what will soon appear as props, or running down the street, as if escaping from his creation. One of these meta-narratives seems to be about looking, specifically clandestine looking or spying, and the other about making, or the role of the artist in relation to his work.

Looking, and making. The concerns that recur through many reflexive arts documentaries of this period are precisely what is normally repressed in normal cinematic spectatorship: the subject who looks and the act of looking as constitutive of its subject; and the materiality and economy of the art process. *Scenes and songs* adds to the iconographic implications of its tableaux an equivalent discourse that is otherwise absent from Webb's gallery work.

Postscript
1983

The decade that separates *Scenes and songs* from *Love story* has seen Webb refine and intensify his *mise en scène*, moving from the mythopoeic to the microscopic, as his imagery becomes

increasingly biological. Sperm, germs, eggs, vulva and penis metaphors are the recurrent motifs of his cibachromes of the early 1990s. Not surprisingly, this biomorphic theme proves central to *Love story*. So too does the fact that it is an animated film, in view of the long and complex relationship between animation and surrealism.

To describe Webb as a surrealist would beg many questions and distinctions. It is perhaps less a matter of definition than interpretation. To penetrate the immaculate, self-contained worlds he conjures, either in macrocosm or in microcosm, we need the resources with which surrealism has equipped us – to dram, to decode, to doodle, to annexe science as well as scatology for poetic purposes. More narrowly, it was the original surrealist group who first grasped the immense potential of cinema to figure many of their concerns and discoveries, and who thereby helped legitimate and inspire the tradition of fantastic cinema which includes animation.

From the pixillated fantasies and frolics of Méliès at the turn of the century to such contemporary three-dimensional animators as Svankmajer and the Quay Brothers, surrealism has provided a key to unlocking the strange fascination of this medium.[10] Animation is, first and foremost, primitive magic realised by modern means: mere marks and objects come to life; all physical laws and human limits are suspended; *anything can happen*. From a surrealist perspective, animation also permits the freest play of desire in search of its goals, however disturbing or absurd. In Starewicz's pioneering puppet films, for instance, insects commit adultery, toys and animals pursue their passions with unrestrained intensity and, conversely, human figures become puppets.[11]

Surrealism delighted in 'found' material, in naive or unconscious embodiments of its themes, which helped to create an appreciation of popular as well as primitive art. In the surrealist pantheon, popular movies, comicstrips, pornography and curiosities of all kinds, mingle with tribal and psychotic art to create a counter-culture, challenging the bourgeois propriety of fine art. So successful was this revolt that we are in constant danger of forgetting how much it prepared the way for many post-World War II developments in art which appear to have no direct link with surrealism. Nor, of course, can the surrealists take sole credit for realising that popular animation embodies something vital, and conspicuously missing from much modern art. Sergei Eisenstein was a devout admirer of Disney from the early 1930s, and while working on *Ivan the Terrible* during the war he wrote of Disney's latest release:

> *Bambi* is already a shift towards ecstasy – serious, eternal: the theme of *Bambi* is the
> circle of life – *the repeating circle of lives*.
> No longer the sophisticated smile of the twentieth century toward totems. But a return
> to pure totemism and a reverse shift towards evolutionary pre-history.
> A humanised deer, or rather, – a 're-deerized' human.[12]

Eisenstein delighted in the idea of comparing his intense historical drama with the protean appeal of Disney's 'absolutely stunning' *Willie the whale*: '…through *Ivan*, I also "read" Willie'.[13]

It isn't difficult to read *Love story* through the lens of surrealism, as it pays ironic tribute to both the surrealist passion for cinema-going and the cult of *amour fou*. The popcorn-spectator that comes to life only in the flickering twilight of the cinema is, after all, a cinephile of sorts – and a victim of chance, when it is abruptly transported to another theatre. It then experiences an appropriately consuming passion as it couples violently with its mate – only for their union to be cut short by a vacuum cleaner which sucks them up into the void, where they hover; star-crossed lovers suspended in a vegetable version of the ecstasy that Eisenstein recognised in Disney.

What no doubt helps the film achieve its pop(corn)-allegory of cinema is the fact that Webb's collaborators were the London satirical animation studio, Spitting Image.[14] This has ensured a slickness and polish, with pounding generic film music, far removed from the eerie stillness of Webb's other work. Coming at the peak of acclaim for British three-dimensional animation, marked by Aardman's world-wide success with **Creature comforts** and the Wallace and Gromit series, **Love story** assumes the guise of a commercial animation short in order to reach its audiences' collective unconscious.

The close relationship between film spectatorship and a surrealist sensibility is explored in **Seeing in the dark**, a highly entertaining 'compendium of cinemagoing' edited by the artists Ian Breakwell and Paul Hammond (the latter also a well-known historian of surrealism in cinema).[15] Granting 'poetic licence in a public place under cover of darkness', cinemagoing is for Breakwell and Hammond and their many contributors 'a collective rite rich in surreal experience'. Two themes that run through the anecdotes, confessions and fantasies in this marvellous collection are the role of chance in disrupting – and often enhancing – the mechanised spectacle of cinema, and the seemingly intrinsic eroticism of the cinema auditorium.

Far from the cinema being a place of passive consumption or mass hypnosis as it has often been stigmatised by the guardians of elitist art, Breakwell and Hammond follow André Breton and many later artists in emphasising how it offers a distinctive new experience, a place of private reverie, self-discovery, exhibitionism, voyeurism, erotic adventure and (according to the title of Hans Richter's surrealist anthology of film) 'dreams that money can buy'.[16] **Love story** distils this quintessentially surrealist insight into a work that continues Webb's exploration of sexually-charged imagery – indeed almost parodies the plasticene spermatozoa of his **Entomb**, **Parole** and **Tutelar** (pp 138, 25, 140), and the condom-like balloons of **Germ** and **Miasma & ampoule** (p 134) – yet places his popcorn lovers in an untypically explicit narrative.

The final image of **Love story**, as the popcorn pair recede into space accompanied by an orgasmic musical climax, clinches the parodic dimension of the film;[17] but it also translates these anthropomorphic figures into a more characteristically ambiguous image. Even as we smile at the **Star wars/Star trek** finale, we can read the image as a typically open Webb metaphor for death-birth/the cell as a universe/inner space-outer space. And to facilitate this reading, in 'Spellbound' Webb exhibited alongside **Love story** a large photographic piece, **Asteroid and kidney stone** (pp 62-63), which uses popcorn imagery against a 'cosmic' Möbius strip. As in **Scenes and songs**, Webb seizes the opportunity offer by a film to extend and deepen the way in which his photographic tableaux are understood. In the memory-cinema of **Love story**, we are encouraged to dream the narratives that swarm around his more usual 'stills'.

For the historic avant-gardes of the 1910s and 1920s, the futurists, dadaists and surrealists, film offered a chance to demonstrate their concerns in a new and dynamic form. Ginna's **Vita futurista**, Bragaglia's **Il perfido incanto**, Picabia's and Clair's **Entr'acte**, Léger's **Ballet mècanique**, Man Ray's **Retour à la raison** and **Emak Bakia**, Duchamp's **Anèmic cinema**, Bunuel and Dali's **Un**

film stills
from
Love story
1996

chien andalou – all these are, in varying degrees, both *jeux d'esprits* and *oeuvres à thèse*. They were made to see what could be done with film, and also to lay claim to the new medium as an extension of art's technical resources. They remained, for the most part, isolated experiments. Seventy-odd years later, much has changed in the relationship between art and cinema, but the same problem – and opportunity – remains. How can independent artists engage with film on their terms, without being taken over by its formidable technical and professional demands?

The tradition of 'artists' films' has been and is likely to remain a precarious one, highly dependent on individual initiatives and chance conjunctions. Thinking about how Boyd Webb has punctuated his career with several works on film leads almost inevitably to the earlier case of Len Lye, a fellow-New Zealand artist who became an 'accidental' film-maker while living in England. And this, more than any speculation about a shared 'New Zealandness', may be a useful way to fix the significance of both Webb's and Lye's otherwise orphaned film work.

Lye reached London in 1926, after working his passage on a boat from Australia, and previously spending a crucial year in Samoa.[18] It was during his time in the South Seas that he began to synthesise a highly personal blend of quasi-anthropological and modernist thinking. From Pacific and Aboriginal tribal art he acquired an interest in decorative pattern and its links with dance, while he also began to study film animation technique in Sydney. When he reached Europe and caught up with the latest experiments in art cinema and abstract animation, he realised the possibility of using ritualistic imagery and rhythm in a new kind of drawn or painted film. The first fruit of this was *Tusalava* **1929**, a scroll-like or totemic work, described by Lye as a 'ritual dance film'.[19]

Although unknown for decades after its premiere at the Film Society, which had funded its completion, *Tusalava* can now been seen as both a highly personal product of Lye's eclectic interests, and a part of the modernist 'graphic film' movement which flourished in the 1920s. Lye hoped to extend *Tusalava* into a trilogy, but was unable to find backing until five years later, when John Grierson proposed that a directly painted abstract film, *Colour box*, might have an advertising slogan and soundtrack added, and be released by the GPO Film Unit. Half a dozen films followed in which Lye explored combinations of rhythm, imagery and the new photographic colour processes, as well as audiovisual counterpoint with the soundtrack. Lye emigrated to New York in 1944, and continued to make occasional films, but poured much of his energy into kinetic sculpture.

The point is not to force a comparison between Webb and Lye, although there are interesting parallels in their biomorphism and points of contact with the surrealist tradition – but to underline how an artist can take film in radically new directions, as Lye did in the mid-1930s; and how, in turn, film can offer the opportunity to create a new kind of 'total' artwork, which will bring together sound, vision, temporality, and new relations of viewing and circulation.

I described Boyd Webb as among the most cinematic of contemporary artists, not because he appears to be a frustrated filmmaker, nor because his stills invoke explicit film references, like Cindy Sherman or Sam Taylor-Wood. He is cinematic more in the sense that Eisenstein regarded Leonardo, Pushkin, Daumier and many pre-cinema artists as making use of similar techniques of construction to those of cinema. As we look at Webb's arranged photographs, we bring to them, like Webb himself, skills of reading that owe much to cinema spectatorship (and indeed to magazine and advertising consumption). Webb clearly counts on this shared universe of filmic discourse; and in his rare, but compelling, film works he draws us further into a cinematic perspective on his stills. Like his fellow 'alchemists of the surreal' every medium his uses endows 'the real – the very materiality of the world: its objects, surfaces and textures – with an aura of strangeness and the fantastic'.[20]

Notes

1   *Spellbound: Art and Film* included Fiona Banner, Terry Gilliam, Douglas Gordon, Peter Greenaway, Damien Hirst, Steve McQueen, Eduardo Paolozzi, Paula Rego, Ridley Scott and Boyd Webb. It was organised by the Hayward Gallery, London, in association with the British Film Institute, and curated by Ian Christie and Philip Dodd, February–April 1996.

2   Fernand Léger and Dudley Murphy, *Ballet mècanique* **1924**; Marcel Duchamp, *Anèmic Cinema* **1924-6**; Luis Bunuel and Salvador Dali, *Un chien andalou* **1929**.

3   A 'Festival of Expanded Cinema' took place at the Institute of Contemporary Arts, London, in January 1976, with work by over forty artists. The catalogue quoted Jonas Mekas identifying London as the most advanced centre of 'expanded cinema' in 1973, and noting that 'the London school is deep into structural researches into process art, and the formal exploration of space relationships'.

4   An historical and contemporary survey of abstract, non-narrative and landscape film. Hayward Gallery, 1979.

5   *The great ice cream robbery* **1971**, about Claes Oldenberg at the Tate Gallery, is intended to be shown on two screens simultaneously; *Chance, history, art* **1979**, was commissioned to record the 1978 Hayward Gallery exhibition, 'Dada and surrealism reviewed'.

6   Among the innovative Arts Council films made at this time were Noel Burch's *Correction please, or how we got into movies* **1979**, on early film form; Keith Griffiths' and the Quays' *The eternal day of Michel de Ghelderode* **1981**; Laura Mulvey and Peter Wollen's *Frida Kahlo and Tina Modotti* **1982**; David Rowan's *The strange case of Marcel Duchamp* **1984**.

7   *The world of Gilbert and George* **1981**. Haas subsequently made *Stones and flies* **1988** with the landscape artist Richard Long, and has since moved into features, with *The music of chance* **1993** and *Angels and insects* **1995**.

8   Among the important new-style opera productions of the 1980s were Patrice Chereau's production of Wagner's *Ring* cycle at Bayreuth, and Peter Sellars' Mozart and Handel stagings in Purchase and Boston.

9   See Hilty, Greg, 'A Degree of Unease: The Work of Boyd Webb', in London: British Council, 1994. *Boyd Webb* (catalogue for the VIII Indian Triennale).

10 See programme for the touring programme, 'Alchemists of the surreal', organised for the British Film Institute by Michael O'Pray, Jayne Pilling and Paul Taylor, 1986; including work by Méliès, Painlevé, Franju, Corman, Borowczyk, Cronenberg, David Lynch, Bunuel, Jeff Keen, Joseph Cornell, Greenaway, Svankmajer and the Quays.

11 See Pilling, J. (ed), 1983. *Starewicz 1882-1965*, Edinburgh International Film Festival.

12 Note headed DISNEY, dated Alma-Ata, 3. 7. 1943; in Leyda, J (ed), *1988. Eisenstein on Disney*, London: Methuen, p 63.

13 ibid.

14 *Love story* was produced by Pam Asbury through the Cairo Studios of Spitting Image, producers of the popular British television satire series of the same name.

15 Breakwell, Ian and Paul Hammond (eds), 1990. *Seeing in the dark*, Serpent's Tail. Paul Hammond is also the author of *Marvellous méliès* (1974) and editor of *The shadow and its shadow* (1978).

16 *Dreams that money can buy* (US, 1946) includes episodes created by Max Ernst, Fernand Léger, Man Ray, Marcel Duchamp, Alexander Calder and Gerhard Richter.

17 Webb originally planned to have soundtrack extracts from recognisable films of many genres.

18 See Auckland City Art Gallery, 1980. *Len Lye: a personal mythology*.

19 Cited in Horrocks, Roger, 'Len Lye's films', in *Len Lye: a personal mythology*, p 27.

20 O'Pray, Michael, *Alchemists of the surreal: the films of Jas Svankmajor and the Brothers Quay*. Catalogue for touring film programme, Film and Video Umbrella, 1986. I am indebted to Michael O'Pray's essay on Boyd Webb's *Love story* in the catalogue *Spellbound: art and film*, Philip Dodd and Ian Christie (eds), 1996.

Dyad
1993

True griffins

Lynne Cooke

I. Pataphysical speculation

> Artists produce their best work indirectly ... It is like juggling a lot of cats in the air – at the right moment they form a rug.
> — Boyd Webb

> ...one likes to recall that the difference between the comic side of things and their cosmic side, depends on one sibilant.
> — Vladimir Nabokov

> I pity the man who can see the connection of his own ideas. Still more do I pity him, the connection of whose ideas any other person can see.
> — Mr. Flosky

In his diatribe against the pettiness of positivist thought and the shortcomings of logical reasoning Mr. Flosky (alias Coleridge) puts the counter-case, for speculative metaphysics, most persuasively.

> The enthusiasm for abstract truth is an exceedingly fine thing, as long as the truth, which is the object of the enthusiasm, is so completely abstract as to be altogether out of reach of the human faculties ...[F]or the pleasure of metaphysical investigation lies in the means, not in the end; and if the end could be found, the pleasure of the means would cease. The proper exercise of the mind is elaborate reasoning. Analytical reasoning is a base and mechanical process, which takes to pieces and examines, bit by bit, the rude material of knowledge, and extracts therefrom a few hard and obstinate things called facts...[unlike] synthetical reasoning, setting up as its goal some unattainable abstraction, like an imaginary quantity in algebra, and commencing its course with taking for granted some two assertions which cannot be proved, from the union of these two assumed truths produces a third assumption, and so on in infinite series. The beauty of the process is, that every step it strikes out in two branches, in a compound ratio of ramification; so that you are perfectly sure of losing your way, and keeping your mind in perfect health, by the perpetual exercise of an interminable quest.[1]

Sharing Flosky's scorn for the nugatory nature of analytical reasoning, compared with the rich lode inherent in synthetic reasoning, the works of Boyd Webb proffer 'perpetual exercise' for the mind in the form of 'an interminable quest'. And if, as Thomas Peacock asserts, the means

Cipher and decipher 1977

to perfect health lie in speculation, this may become, in its highest form, a branch of metaphysics.

Until the seventeenth century Christianity provided a convincing and comprehensive world-view for the West, and the tenets of Christian thought constituted the base for meditation. When science replaced religion as the source of absolute and immutable truths, philosophy and science converged and metaphysical speculation took root there. With the undermining of religion as the basis and origin of a settled account of humanity's place in the universe, science attained a pre-eminence and sovereignty that has remained unvanquished – though not unchallenged, as Flosky/Coleridge's panegyric attests – into the twentieth century.

In recent years, however, the discrediting of one supposed scientific law after another has revealed science's alleged truths to be neither absolute nor universal, but, at best, provisional and hypothetical. Their credibility resides not in their claims to immutability but in their serviceability, since if any theory admits of alternatives, all are reduced to the status of equivalent descriptions. The instability of knowledge, together with the short sell-by date of most of the premises on which a world-view might be constructed, have produced a state of cognitive uncertainty, a loss of authority and a concomitant growth in scepticism which now open the doors to alternative accounts or postulates which attempt to bridge the gap. Science has thus not only relinquished its claim to objective immutable truth but, given their complex and arcane terminologies, the languages in which it is shaped and articulated, it is decreasingly related to ordinary life and interpersonal relationships. And, to the degree that it has forfeited its credibility and its availability as the basis for a comprehensive and exhaustive world-view, analytical reasoning has been eclipsed, while synthetic reasoning gains viability such that metaphysical speculation today occupies new ground.

Boyd Webb's work demonstrates his abiding – albeit ambivalent – interest in science. Yet he is as fascinated with its foibles as its successes, with its bastards as well as its legitimate progeny. Thus, in his world palmistry, alchemy, angelology and astrology coexist on an equal footing with zoology, physics and microbiology. A number of his early works, from the mid-seventies, focussed on some of the more preposterous, but not implausible, ways by which the layperson attempts to come to terms with the fundamental tenets of science or with its underlying premises. In *Approaching the equator* **1976**, for example, the two passengers lean over the sides of their respective deck-chairs instead of the ship's rails, as most passengers reputedly do, in their equally futile attempt to observe the crossing of the line. While in *First principles* **1985** (p 112), some absolute law, perhaps to do with gravity or its suspension, seems to be enacted with the aid of happenstance props.

Webb's method typically consists of according an elaborate staging, which is patently fictive and generally makeshift in character, the status of truth by the 'honesty' implied in the 'straight' use of photography for 'objective', impartially documented, statements. Photography is employed in part as proof of authenticity: by accepting the manifest content – the reality of what is depicted – the viewer is led inevitably to embrace the latent content – the fantasy generated by these contingent or adventitious props. It is this paradoxical coupling of overt falsity or absurdity with unqualified, naïve verisimilitude that renders these early visions so compelling. In seeking to give form to, but not 'explain', the unknowable, the ungraspable and the intractably abstract, Webb devises means which are akin to those employed by medieval illuminators who similarly sought to depict the miraculous and spectacular through the familiar and quotidian. Thus God's intervention, for example, may be represented as a hand reaching out of a cloud, or the forest by two large leaves on stalks; and layers of cloth with manifold curls and pleats create the topography of heaven and earth. Parallels are frequently encountered in Webb's work, as in *Lung* **1983** (p 51), where the seas are composed from a large strip of rippling blue carpet, or in *Supplicant* **1984** (p 89), where a woman ensconced in the voluminous folds of a majestic rug addresses the cosmos through a megaphone. And in *Nemesis* **1983** (p 87), the implosion of a toy house by an invading balloon vividly embodies our conviction, however irrational and ludicrous, that power resides in an inexplicable, superhuman, undiscoverable force that destroys from within, power that, as the title hints, might correspond to a form of retributive justice.

The growing specialisation, technicality, complexity and speed of change in contemporary science render it increasingly obscure to the layperson, notwithstanding the plethora of infotainment – popular books, magazine articles, and media programmes designed to render comprehensible, palatable and even entertaining what otherwise resists apprehension and easy assimilation. Of these highly abstruse subjects none enthrals more than astronomy – or astrophysics as it is now more properly termed. Once the province of science fiction, outer space has recently taken on the character of something like a neighbouring domain inhabited by black holes and other cosmic phenomena of which we speak with comfortable, even casual familiarity. The models, diagrams, charts and other visualisations proliferating in journals, paperback books, CD ROMs, cult texts and television specials, hypothesise incredible magnitudes of distance, time and space with disarming simplicity. But in the end they only impart a pseudo-knowledge, which is superficial and specious. Moreover, compared with the speculative metaphysics that former eras discovered in cosmology, these most recent forms of information too often seem paltry, meagre, uncertain and lacklustre in their fixation on mensuration and material causality. Alternative accounts are sought constantly, from sources as diverse as New Age thinkers and occult revivals. Because they are bolder and more ambitious, such modes of visualising and conceptualising frequently prove more emotively persuasive.

In a series of works from the mid-1980s loosely focused on astronomy, Webb presents a cosmos which is compellingly seductive and alluring, an equivalent in contemporary guise and imaginative richness of the cosmologies of medieval times. With the antinomies of artifice and reality, the real and the illusory, with strangeness and naturalness held in abeyance, and all certainties undermined, an intermediate zone is opened up, recalling that between playing and reality, dreaming and waking experience. Following the medieval illuminator who employed certain mundane objects that were to hand as his props, Webb also commandeers commonplace paraphernalia, including globes, maps, fruitcake and asparagus; and they are likewise required to play new roles, to act metonymically or to serve as indices to something larger, beyond the normal limits of the discourse. Given the vastness and enormity of outer space, the immensity of scales which defy comprehension, why should a slice of fruitcake or a bunched napkin, for example, not prove useful means of visualising the unobservable?

If readers accept without demur the grainy, blurred photographs captured by some distant satellite of an even more remote heavenly body, how much more compelling will be Webb's renderings of the solar system. Whilst no trickery is apparent in the satellite's photographs, they have little of the potency, immediacy and hypnotic legibility, and consequently convey few of the imaginative satisfactions, of Webb's eloquent visualisations. Devoid of all possibility of further disclosure by amateurs and the untrained, the astrophysicists' photographs ultimately pall. In Webb's art, by contrast, the manifest falsity is so disarmingly stated that it is quickly passed over: they quickly take on the role of dioramas projecting a hypothetical future.

Because so candidly present, contradiction and artifice neither undermine the potency of the image nor require resolution. Thus these images admit of neither falsity nor verification; their truth-value approximates to that pertaining to most scientific hypotheses which need only be internally self-regulating, consistent and transforming. Yet the quasi-scientific speculation they galvanise does not preclude them from having also the status of religious belief. Just as we respect and recognise the potency and sacred identity of artefacts from other cultures, without necessarily being able to enter into their belief systems, so in Webb's art we intuit and empathise with the operations of cosmologies quite alien to our own. Seeing is not believing, for we believe and yet do not, in one and the same movement. For the Protestant in the eucharist the substances of the body and blood of Christ co-exist in union with the bread and wine, while in contrast, for the Catholic transubstantiation means that the substances of bread and wine are no longer present, only their 'accidents' persist.

Webb's work is thus as far from subjective fantasy as it is from the realm of science fiction. It is not the bizarre and incongruous, nor the implausible and weird that he courts, but convincing visualisations of what we think we know or understand but can only grasp haltingly, and often with the most ludicrous and uncanny aids. Since there is no mystery as to 'how' (for nothing in the making is concealed), nor 'why' (for all is obvious if not rationally explicable) questions relating to 'how' and 'why' are quickly replaced by a ready acceptance, the necessary basis for encouraging speculation and meditation, the ultimate goal of Webb's art.

Decoy
1986

Webb's first works, which often took the form of tableaux and scenarios, led to him being dubbed a dramatist of the absurd. The works from the early 1980s onwards, by contrast, have a more monumental, elliptical and abbreviated character: no longer moments wrenched out of a continuous narrative they seem visions of an eternal present, outside duration. And, where formerly meaning was conveyed through intricate visual and verbal punning, permeated with a spirit of enigmatic theatricality, a quieter, more poetic idiom, imbued with an ineffable logic of its own, now reigns. Yet the sense of indubitable rightness they convey need not exclude some element of strangeness, as found in *Medallion* **1986** (p 107), nor capriciousness, as in *Torque* **1986**. The characteristic refrain is nonetheless more often one of poignancy, melancholy, wistfulness or yearning. In *Decoy* **1986** (previous page), for example, the tiny flag/plant seems to attract the attention of some passing celestial body with a pathos more riveting than the overweening rhetoric that accompanied the depositing of the American flag in the moon's soil at the close of the 1960s.

Webb's simulated reality is arguably no less believable than the actual one that was relayed by satellite to television screens around the globe.

Although his modified realities strain plausibility they never completely undermine credibility. Is the paper globe sliding dizzily along some treacly milky way in *Excursion* **1986**, any more outlandish than the images conjured in our casual talk of star wars, white dwarves and black holes, or by the now outdated classroom experiments with oranges and ping-pong balls used as surrogates for planets, or even by the Romanesque painter's depiction of the sun drawn across the heavens by a chariot and horses? Confronted with the fact that subatomic particles and electromagnetic radiation, for instance, can be understood only as theoretical constructs, being open neither to observation not to verification, the suspicion arises that even in those areas which are subject to observation and verification our understanding may be no greater. However illusory Webb's world, it is inhabited by objects whose surfaces, textures, colour and mass are manifestly factual and whose presence seems undeniable. He, in short, makes the unbelievable believable.

In his sceptical, selective approbation of science as in his highly compressed poetic transformations, Webb betrays an affinity with Alfred Jarry, whose writings he much admires. Jarry's pataphysics, variously defined as 'the science of imaginary solutions', 'the science of laws governing exceptions', or 'a calamitous science of physics', is an entrancing, bewildering arena for hypothetical speculation. His aberrant blend of scientific and theological speculation, his anarchic humour, his hypnotic visions marked by limpidity and an extreme lucidity, and his proclivity for terse episodic narrative, have echoes in Webb's art and aesthetic.[2] Sufi tales also provide an important source of inspiration for they offer a succinct, enchanting story that fascinates by its elliptical twists of fate and gnomic meanings.[3] Equally importantly, like their counterparts in other cultures, these parables instruct while they entertain.

Microbiology rather than astronomy became a key subject for Webb in the mid-1990s. With their minute sections of matter apparently magnified thousands of times, this series becomes the contrary counterpart to the cosmologies in which the vast reaches of outer space were shrunk to the limits of the manageable. In this group of works the three-dimensional yet shallow stage-set particular to the diorama has been replaced by panoramic slices of matter which, in their semi-translucent, wafer-thin state, recall the way a specimen is delivered to a microscope as a slice or sliver. Dramatised into lurid and luscious surfaces of the kind found in *Donor* **1994** (p 142), or *Nonage* **1995** (pp 152-153), these organic substances recall bodily fluids subject to intense scrutiny. Divested of all narrative or episodic traces, they become haunting, autonomous universes. Ultimately, however, it is less their autonomy than the fact that, ironically, they appear so unreachable which makes them so insidiously disturbing.

Both microscopic photography and that which maps the solar system depend on forms of magnification in order to make visible material that can never be confirmed by the unaided human observer. Although these prostheses have opened up worlds previously unavailable to the naked eye, increasingly imaging has become, according to Lisa Cartwright, a more central means of diagnosis, and sensory perception, including sight, is progressively destabilised as a source of knowledge.[4] In this way inscriptions of data produced through technology replace the sensory observations of the scientist as a privileged source of information. As the dependency on technology grows so there is a corresponding dispersal of embodied sight. Perception becomes unhinged from the sensory body only to be enacted across an increasingly complex battery of institutional techniques and instruments.

It is arguably not fortuitous that Webb has been drawn to these arenas in which new imaging modalities prevail. At the very sites where data inscription, analysis and instrumental regulation are foregrounded over the act of observation he proposes a counter: the psychical

Distressed hose
1980

spaces of the inner eye. In this, he builds on Freud's celebrated comparison of those 'ideal points' at which the image in these prostheses comes into being with the locus of psychic reality:

> We should picture the instrument which carries out our mental functions, as resembling a compound microscope or a photographic apparatus or something of the kind. On that basis psychical locality which corresponds to a point inside the apparatus at which one of the preliminary stages of an image comes into being. In the microscope and telescope as we know, these occur in parts at ideal points, regions in which no tangible component to the apparatus is situated.[5]

As Jonathan Crary persuasively argues, contemporary visual practices increasingly alienate the human observer. 'Most of the historically important functions of the human eye are being supplanted by practices in which visual images no longer have any reference to an observer in a 'real', optically perceived world,' Crary contends.[6] 'If these images can be said to refer to anything,' he continues, in terms highly relevant to Webb's practice, 'it is to millions of bits of electronic mathematical data. Increasingly, visuality will be situated on a cybernetic and electromagnetic terrain where abstract visual and linguistic elements coincide and are consumed, circulated and exchanged globally'.[7] Webb's disdain for the computer as an aid to his image making is thus deeply grounded in his aesthetic: in these recent works the psychic truth of the inner eye infiltrates the very heart of the new imaging modalities.

Webb implies that not only are our certainties and convictions frequently unfounded, flawed and unreliable but that, too often, they are imaginatively impotent and metaphysically impoverished as well. Poetical speculation must become the real counterpart and complement to the research and hypothetical reasoning of modern science. Since the question of the literal truth or falsity of his photographic propositions gives way before their imaginative potency and eloquence, they might best be described as 'true griffins'. John Ruskin famously distinguished between true and false griffins by comparing two renderings of the beast, a medieval Lombard variant and a classical one. Countering the assertion that 'There never were such beasts', he argued that, 'The difference is, that the Lombard workman really did see a griffin in his imagination, and carved it from the life, meaning to declare to all ages that he had verily seen with his immortal eyes such a griffin as that; but the classical workman never saw a griffin at all, nor anything else; but put the whole thing together by line and rule'.[8] It seems fitting to Webb's mode of thought that a New Zealander should become the modern counterpart of this Lombard predecessor.

An age that apotheosises materialist philosophy, positivist proof and the dictates of logic, an age that is devoted to analytical discursive reasoning, far too often fails to address the issue of revelation. With the shortcomings of science currently all too evident, the realm of speculative metaphysics in which visual and verbal poetics constitute the pre-eminent languages, takes on a new potency and resonance. By giving full reign to imaginative and purposeless speculation, Webb suggests that we can begin to approach 'perfect health' and redress the balance against empty rationalising and materialist explanations of the kind that Flosky abhorred. To make sense of a baffling, contrary universe different theories and postulates need to be regarded not as competing or conflicting accounts but as co-existent recipes for eliciting compatible but alternative conclusions.

II. Averted vision

The traditional aesthetics and conventions of photography don't interest me. I use photography because it is an essential fact of the age and I believe that an artist should use the materials and techniques of his time. Photography is a flexible medium, capable of being stretched in many directions. Tolerant of much abuse it always retains an inherent honesty – it can reproduce with great clarity even the most featureless of man-made materials. I make use of this integrity to reflect a certain moral uprightness that I hope lies at the core of my work.
— Boyd Webb

It was more by default than design that photography became Boyd Webb's preferred medium. 'I started as a sculptor making life casts of people in fibreglass and arranging them in tableaux. But it was an expensive and cumbersome practice. The need to record them led me to photography. With photography I could use actors, arranging them at will. I had complete control'.[9] In adopting photography initially as a recording device Webb aligned himself with much current practice within that large and amorphous terrain known as conceptual art. In the

Lung
1983

late 1960s photography had entered the realms of fine art practice through the back door as it were, as a humble tool or a supporting medium for witnessing events, actions and performances whose ephemeral nature or dispersed locations made them otherwise unavailable to an audience. In the work of Bruce McLean, for example, it offered not only dispassionate testimony but an unprecedented immediacy in capturing the evanescent moment that was the focus of a series of subversive actions staged outdoors. McLean produced small black and white prints of these actions, in which it was irrelevant whether the artist or someone acting at his instigation had pressed the shutter. It was the amateur ethos that mattered in these revised versions of reportage. For this very amateurishness was regarded as further testimony to their authenticity as records. Consequently McLean's prints, like Webb's photography, were neither art works *per se*, nor subject to the kinds of critical issues that marked the discourse of art photography proper.

If other contemporary British artists, such as John Hilliard, did investigate in self-conscious and rigorous fashion the medium itself, still others, among whom Gilbert and George were notable, turned to photography's alternative tradition – as a studio practice. Rather than a passive record of the fleeting world at large, studio photography ceded directorial control to the image maker. More than a witness, the camera now became the vehicle through which the work was made (though paradoxically, in the case of Gilbert and George, the results were termed sculpture not photography). In such series as **Cherry blossoms 1974**, for example, the arch, stylised character of the Living Sculptures' behaviour was devised explicitly for the camera, then reinforced by the overprinting of the then mandatory black and white print with a lurid red wash.

In adopting a directorial stance, Webb became automatically affiliated with the tradition of studio photography, yet from the beginning his stance was singular and, characteristically, contrary. Not only did he choose to work in colour, then held in high suspicion, but he parodied other received notions. Among his earliest mature statements, **Herbert Groves 1973** (p 69), for example, juxtaposes two quite unexceptional images, one a banal genre photograph, the second akin to the illustrations found in medical textbooks. One detail, however, proves unsettling. Instead of the forceps that would customarily be used to prop open the mouth, the instruments employed here seem suspiciously like domestic meat skewers. The type of photographic images utilised in **Herbert Groves** would normally serve to give credence to a disturbing story, the abnormal condition, which is recounted here, as is appropriate, in as dry and impersonal a tone as possible to indicate the absence of any distortion or embroidery of the 'facts'. Yet the untoward detail of the maverick forceps undermines the scientific demeanour of the whole approach, introducing a capricious, subversive note, one which then ricochets throughout the piece so that the impartial documentary probity of the medium itself comes to seem at risk. In turn, the juxtaposition of the kind of furtive snapshot surreptitiously gleaned by, say, a forensic investigator with the carefully posed image required in medical research comes to seem increasingly improper, and unconvincing: the two types of evidence prove strangely incompatible. The paradoxical result is that the evidential character of photography itself seems called into question rather than the plausibility of the case study.

The studio format asserted itself more directly and insistently in many of the works which followed over the next two years. The majority of these tableaux were shot against a

Denizen
1989

paper backdrop which, in removing any sense of place, further dramatised the *mise en image*. With the exception of ***The mandatory second opinion* 1977** (p 76), where Webb employed a wide-angle lens to heighten the impact of the foreshortened desktop, and introduced concealed lighting to dramatise its elephantine massive legs, he rigorously eschewed any manipulation of the mechanism or of the print in order to make the objects read as factually as possible, and hence the image appears as believable as possible.

Since a diptych format offered greater narrative possibilities than a single image, very often Webb used it to tease out the frustration or bafflement that ensued from simultaneously extending and truncating the report or situation. In ***Prehensile torpor* 1977** (p 77), for example, two views of the same scene are offered, as if 'before' and 'after'. Yet denouement can hardly be said to have been effected, for, although the woman's missing shoe is recovered in the second image, she collapses, prone, now clutching a drawing whose mysterious significance further complicates the situation. Though suggesting duration, as many new questions are introduced as answers vouchsafed.

The use of colour, and of a heightened palette in particular, had been anathema to most conceptual artists. Webb's recourse to these tools did not align him, however, with more conventional or mainstream photographic practices. Defined by curving and arcing edges, the idiosyncratic formats of many of his early prints, together with their small scale and deadpan tenor removed them equally from the realms of advertising, fashion photography, pornography and related mass media modes. The blandishments offered by the medium are seldom exploited except in the treatment of light, which like that utilised in much advertising, has a non-directional pervasiveness and a seductive tone, in order that desire enhance deception. Given this combination of scale, palette, lighting and composition (formulaic if maverick genres scenes) these works could almost be mistaken for the kind of mass-produced photograph then designed to decorate domestic settings: something between a calendar reproduction and a Sunday painting. For Webb, their liminal status and ambiguous, elusive identity served to ensure that these 1970s works, like those of most conceptual photographers, skirted the bounds of art photography, with its long-standing focus on seriousness, expertise and reflexiveness, at the same time as they stayed firmly outside the conventional fine art categories of painting and sculpture.

In the early 1980s Webb adopted the format he has continued to use to the present. Enlarging the size of the print to approximately a metre and a half on its longer side ensured that the image was imbued with a presence, a monumentality, and a legibility over a distance, all of which removed it from the realm of the traditional fine art photograph. In addition, forswearing matting and framing in favour of suspending the print by pins from its four corners, he enhanced an appreciation of its object character.

Thus Webb's work of the early 1980s in many ways maintained stronger affinities with that of certain of his peers who were sculptors than it did with fellow artists in Britain who concentrated on photography, such as Olivier Richon. For, by the beginning of the decade Webb had replaced his former tableaux inhabited by actors and props with more fully invented worlds, worlds he created by painting and constructing the components from materials salvaged from domestic settings or hardware stores. His distinctive brand of elliptical, mordant humour, his enigmatic yet unmistakably moral preoccupations and his tendency to juxtapose images further linked his work to that of Bill Woodrow and Richard Wentworth, in particular, among the generation of sculptors then emerging in England.

Increasingly, however, and in contradistinction to the situation that had faced his predecessors, the status and classification of his works – whether as sculpture or as photography – proved irrelevant.[10] For Webb's practice was most appropriately seen within a wider international context, one which encompassed numerous artists working in the arena of studio photography, from Cindy Sherman to Jeff Wall to Fischli and Weiss. Common to the practices of all these artists was a certain level of technical competence in contrast to the high level of expertise found among art photographers on the one hand and on the other the deliberate amateurishness of most 1970s conceptualists who sought a perfunctory, even snapshot idiom.

Shell shock **1983** (p 82), marks this new highpoint in Webb's oeuvre. It depicts a world unto itself for the last traces of the neutral rooms, with their junctions of floor and wall within which the *mise en scene* was previously constructed, have been removed. It is at once fully illusionistic and unexpectedly cohesive, yet still clearly fictitious. It also abandons the overtly handpainted and handmade constructions of the type found in *Laurentian* **1981**, and *Kiss* **1982** (p 83), which juxtaposed various types and levels of illusionism. And, tellingly, it also foregoes the quasi-surrealist mode which seeks to assert incongruity by bringing together disparate items which, as Michel Foucault has demonstrated, is invested with its own unique power to evoke enchantment.

Many of Webb's works from the mid-1980s onwards may be described as landscapes, notwithstanding the fact that some like *Nemesis* **1983** (p 87), include their ostensible makers or manipulators who inhabit an adjacent, usually subterranean zone below. Typically, they turn that most placid, anodyne genre into something uncanny, disquieting or strangely haunting. Generally, such works are composed in shallow planes beyond which the space opens into atmospheric depth, which is conveyed by means of painterly illusion. Restricting sharp focus and detail to the foreground components endows them with a materiality and immediacy that, given the limitations inherent in the camera, would otherwise be difficult to produce. 'The format and physical laws of photography provide a discipline I find inspiring', Webb stated in 1983.[11] While true, it could nonetheless be argued that photography *per se* was not his primary interest, any more than landscape was his preferred subject. Exploiting its potential to establish the most precise and succinct incongruity, the *trompe l'oeil* verisimilitude of photography becomes, in his hands, a means to revitalise the diorama, the nineteenth century's most persuasive and beloved means of constructing a world in miniature.

Thus for all that they observe conventional rules of good composition, clarity and balance, Webb's works situate themselves outside the aesthetic discourse of photography as an art practice. That is, as photography their primary focus lies in galvanising narrative fantasy, a point of view that conforms closely with Pierre Bourdieu's celebrated sociologically- based analysis of the medium.[12] For Bourdieu, photographic judgement is typically not about value but about identity, in that it is a judgement that reads things generically, as landscapes, portraits, and so on: that is, as stereotypes. Invoking such familiar models Webb substitutes quirky variants that call our routine understanding of the world into question, and consequently problematise received information. At the same time he relies on our unquestioning acceptance of photography as a transparent medium, as inherently 'honest', while surreptitiously making full use of its capacity for duplicity. For photography creates rather than recreates the world: it does not capture reality, it fabricates its own. As Susan Sontag avows, 'In the very creation of a duplicate world, of a reality in the second degree, narrower but more dramatic than the one perceived by natural vision', the photographic enterprise conceals a lurking surrealism at its very core.[13] In this enchanted condition, it produces the effect of a condensed, distilled, and intensified world in a miniaturised state, one which echoes that milieu integral to the diorama. In this way, as Ralph Rugoff argues, the camera may be seen as a vitrine.[14] The preternatural hallucinatory stillness of Webb's miniature landscapes, infused with the profound calm of a parallel world gone forever or yet to exist, recalls the typical ambience of their stage set predecessors.

Nowhere is this more intensely evident than in the series of apocalyptic works Webb created at the end of the 1980s, among which *Corral, Chattels, Undrained, Mezzanine* (pp 126, 118, 130), and the sublime *Denizen* (p 53), are particularly memorable. Where most museums of natural history offer visions of an unrecoverable and unwitnessed prehistory, Webb contrarily proffers, with an equally narcotic intensity, glimpses of a dystopian future. Yet in contrast to the dispassionate ways in which these museums confidently recast unknowable past epochs, Webb assumes a deliberately moral stance, as much warning as prophecy. The convention of presenting a diorama under glass makes theirs an orphaned reality. Webb's images, too, lie outside present time, but in place of the sense of suspension in a lost moment encountered in the diorama, these worlds seem trapped between the present and the future, at once visionary and hyperreal. The viscerality and vividness of the print counter the melancholy of the imagery. But this unsettling tension derives equally from their temporal contradictions, for these images can no more be safely allocated to the past, when the negative was shot, than to a future endlessly deferred by the freezing of the image in a single moment. Not only does Webb here astutely exploit the inherent character of this medium, but he capitalises on the fact that photography can be imbued with a contemporaneity the diorama lacks. In Webb's hands photography invests this nineteenth century model with a new level of believability and timeliness, while simultaneously divesting it of its aura of nostalgia.

In this elaborate system of feedback, authenticity becomes wholly a function of the photographically produced reality effect. Thus it becomes irrelevant, for example, that Webb's animals are neither real nor stuffed, but plastic inflatables designed to aid children learning to swim. (Indeed, in a mad but characteristic twist of logic, it may indicate why some manage to swim.) In this way they invest a frequently articulated position with an unexpected moral rectitude: 'Unbelievable and believable have become the same thing. Any viewpoint is as good as any other. They used to call it relativity and now they call it the closest thing to the real thing'.[15] If the simulacrum of the photographic image no longer seems any less real than that of other kinds of experience, it is perhaps because we are now attuned, inescapably and to an unprecedented degree, to the mediated character of all experience. As primary sources are inevitably displaced by their mediated derivatives, belief in the objective fact of a natural world existing somewhere out there has faded to a vague memory. Yet as Flosky/Coleridge asserted and as Webb's works compellingly testify, for all its tenuousness such belief, a mandatory requisite for perfect health, is urgently required.

Notes

1   Peacock, Thomas Love, 1818. *Nightmare abbey*. Harmondsworth: Penguin, 1974, p 67.

2   See, for example, his essay, 'How to construct a time machine', in Shattuck, Roger and Simon Watson Taylor (eds), 1980. *Selected works of Alfred Jarry*. London: Eyre Methuen, p 114-121.

3   Webb's principal sources for these were publications by Idries Shah, notably, *The way of the Sufi*. Harmondsworth: Penguin, 1974.

4   Cartwright, Lisa, 1995. *Screening the body: tracing medicine's visual culture*. Minneapolis: University of Minnesota Press.

5   Freud, Sigmund. *The interpretation of dreams*. cited in Cartwright, op. cit., p 7.

6   Crary, Jonathan, 1990. *Techniques of the observer: on vision and modernity in the nineteenth century*. Cambridge, Mass: MIT Press, p 2.

7   ibid.

8   Ruskin, John, 1898. *Modern painters vol. III*. London.

9   Cited in *Boyd Webb*. Eindhoven: Van Abbemuseum, 1983 (exhibition catalogue). p 11.

10 By the beginning of the 1980s photography was well established as a viable vehicle for sculptors in Britain, not least because of the activities of such self-proclaimed practitioners as Richard Long, Hamish Fulton, and Gilbert and George, all of whom were now producing large-scale, slick, monumental photographs deemed sculpture, and all of whom refused to participate in group shows devoted to photography.

11 Cited in *Boyd Webb*, loc. cit.

12 Bourdieu, Pierre, 1965. *Photography: a middle-brow art*. Stanford CA: Stanford University Press, 1990.

13 Sontag, Susan, 1990. *On photography*. New York: Anchor Books, p 152.

14 Rugoff, Ralph, 1996. 'Half dead'. *Parkett*. no 46, p 133.

15 Prince, Richard, 1983. 'Anyone who is anyone'. *Parkett*. no 6, p 67.

HOLOTHURIANS

script for video tape made July 1974

A man is seated at a table with paper, fountain pen and a bottle of ink.

He begins to write ...

Holothurians or Sea Cucumbers are the most common of mud eating animals found on the deep sea floor. They skim only the very topmost millimeter of recent sediment from the sea bed using tentacles surrounding the mouth. Sediment is continually ingested, collected in the intestine and periodically ejected, as the Holothurians graze the timeless ooze of the abyss.

Slowly the ink becomes fainter and the pen runs dry. The pen is then carefully refilled by unscrewing the barrel revealing the rubber sac. The nib is immersed in the ink, and the rubber sac is repeatedly squeezed and released until the pen is replenished. The barrel is then replaced and the writing continues ....

The small Apodia, Leptosnapta Inhaerens, ejects its faeces with great force. These small animals shrink to one third of their original length at the end of the violent discharge, during which the excrement is thrown distances equivalent to two to eight time its body length. The initial discharge produces spirals while the closing stages produce more loosely looped coils.

end of tape.

Conversation

Boyd Webb and Ron Brownson

Ron Brownson

Can we range over a number of times in your life? Firstly, your time at art school in Christchurch. I heard your final exhibition caused quite a stir.

Boyd Webb

I produced work that the staff did not see until the day of the degree show. Normally in art schools, tutors assess work they are thoroughly familiar with, work which they've seen laboured over all year. On the day, it is given a final polish and presented. I wanted the element of surprise to be an integral part of the work. I produced two bodies of work, one they saw me making and another made in secret and kept under wraps until the big day. The work was locked in a filing cabinet in my 'office' and could only be seen by making an appointment with the secretary I had hired for the day. They came to the door where there was a notice saying they should come back during office hours. It worked very well – they had never been treated so cavalierly.

RB　　Who taught you? Did you have a mentor? How did you become involved in conceptual art practice?

BW　　When I was first at Canterbury, the sculpture department was run by Eric Doudney, whose field was the Romanesque. His idea of sculpture was modelling. Later Tom Taylor, who seemed far more up to date, modernised the course allowing us most of our enthusiasms as long as we could justify what we made. Construction was Tom Taylor's bag, and – like most student work – mine was conceived in a spirit of rebellion.

RB　　Were there any exhibits of conceptual art in Christchurch?

BW　　No, We had a few visits from artists like John Panting and Stephen Furlonger, although not conceptualists, they were from London and very exotic and influential. There were some staff and student exchange exhibitions with Elam. We didn't get any international exhibitions at all, although I do remember a Rodin show. Conceptual art came from magazines. *Studio International* and *Artforum* would appear in the library and we'd pounce on them desperate for the next big thing. Whatever's current is current, and the past is not so interesting. I think at that time art magazines were more influential than anything. Not actual art, but magazines. They were from the other side of the world and full of amazing new ideas. We'd try and knock up a few ourselves. In Christchurch we organised a couple of exhibitions in the new Canterbury Society of Arts Gallery. The shows upset the locals – that's just what students do.

RB   In your work, words have been really important. You've spoken about the notion of titles, names, and words in association with images.

BW   Titles are essential. I think I've made three **Untitled** works altogether and even then the 'Untitled' is qualified with some descriptive attachment in brackets. The pure form of text-only concept art always seemed too bloodless for me. What I strive for is a satisfying resonant amalgam of word and image.

RB   Do you use words to initiate the ideas and issues that you're dealing with?

BW   Yes, in the sense that language is rudimentary to the formation of any idea and, no, in that I generally start with the faintest twinge of an idea. After a period of fiddling and fettling, an amalgam of image and title emerges. To take the dental metaphor further, the work begins to sing (if I am lucky) when the massaged amalgam fits the cavity and toothsomeness is restored. I like the sound of words and if the sound fits the image as well as the meaning an elegantly fragrant *frisson* develops. When fully resolved the pieces should read like an opera, a total ensemble. If you stir all the ingredients and increase the volume they meld into something wondrous, the image, the scale, the colour. See a room full and it's positively quadraphonic – it's a simple wish, but that's how I like them to be seen.

RB   When you're thinking through works like **Smother** (p 133) that have such evocative titles, does the making of the set happen at the same time as the thinking through the echoes of the word?

BW   In the case of **Smother**, the futon and the title were inseparable from birth, but generally there are no rules. The rudiments of the title are there with the germ of the idea.

RB   What did you do when you arrived in England?

BW   In New Zealand, European culture is rather diluted and second-hand. When I got to England, I was dazzled by the richness and diversity of the real thing. While at the Royal College, my work was mainly short hand-written texts illustrated obliquely with colour photographs. The subject matter was provided by my touristic activities

Hello
1987

in London. Christchurch may have been Christchurch, but London was London! The man with the serious case of fungus in his mouth (**Herbert Groves**, p 69) was the first piece I made as a student in 1973. I searched South London for a betting shop with an air extraction vent in the window, to help with the notion of air providing sustenance for fungus. The text's illustrated in a medical manner. I made special tools to hold the man's lips apart and dyed sphagnum moss with food colouring to place in his mouth. I wanted things to be plausible, but only just. They operate in that essentially human zone where things slide from fact to fiction and back again.

RB   There was a time where you used figures and then they disappeared.
For me, the figures don't know whether they are coming, going, arriving or leaving. They are static, yet there's always this potential. How did you pose those figures?

BW   With great difficulty! The actors in those pictures represented everyman or woman and as such they required a universality in their appearance and actions. In most, the gaze is averted to keep the persona neutral. The 'not knowing what they are up to' is probably due to boredom induced by my process – having to repeat the

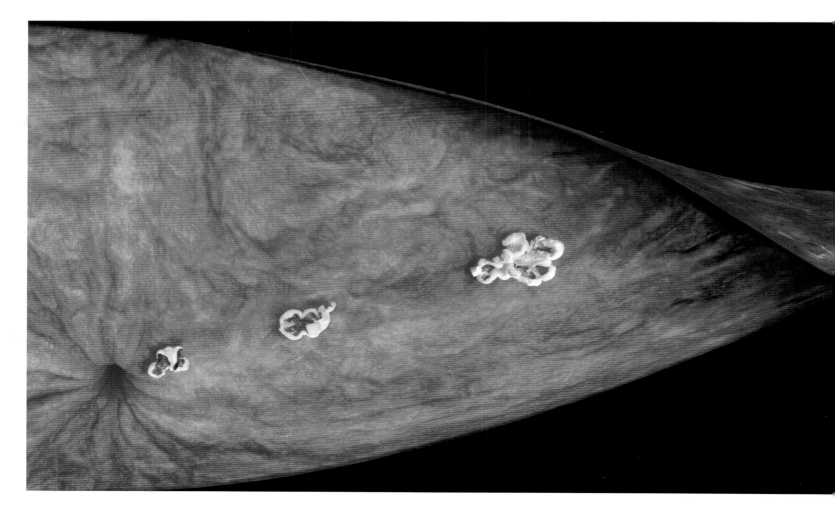

session each time I thought of some slight improvement. In that sense they're completely artificial – staged photo-events.

RB   Fabrications.

BW   That too. There's nothing left to chance. I like to arrange everything. Studio-based work allows that degree of control. As with most camera work, lighting is everything. I was aiming for a very flat, shadowless light that seemed to emanate from the scene itself. A non-photographic light that would enable the picture to have the veracity of a photograph and yet not obviously be a photograph. I wanted something non generic, non specific – an image. Early on I used artificial materials: lino, carpet and underlay, especially the back side which has a lumpen, light-absorbing presence. On close inspection, it is possible to see in the pictures what the materials are and, at the same time, what they are posing as. The combination of these qualities with the title gives a slipperiness to the meaning. The most successful can't be pinned down. They exist in a state of limbo and are memorable in that the mirage of meaning is always shimmering just out of reach – another trick of the light.

Asteroid and kidney stone
1996

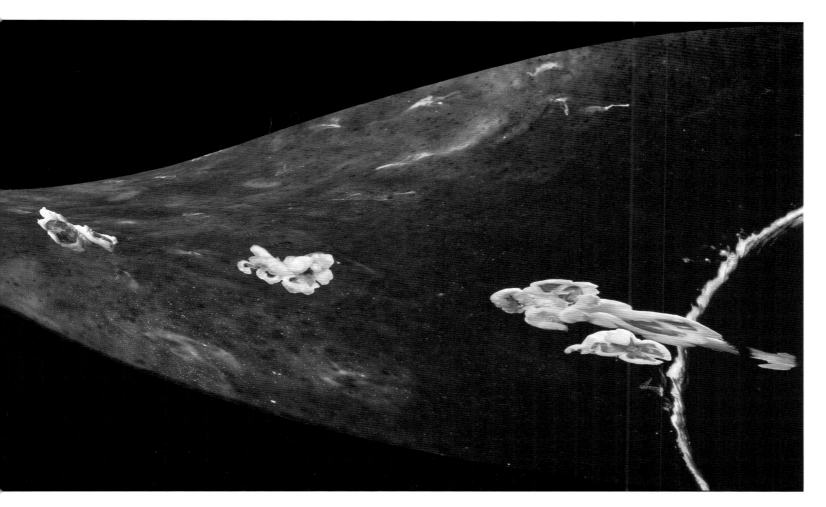

RB There's this journey in your work from the domestic to the vernacular to the quotidian. You slough off the resonance's of domesticity but use the domestic object in a votive action. Votive in the sense of equivocal human expression. You've picked up some series of objects, and stuck them together in association that you would never see at home.

BW The wish to take the domestic into realms beyond the imaginable seems to me to be a truly human aspiration.

RB Recognising what hasn't been seen before.

BW Artists are licensed to dream, to imagine the unimaginable. To be an artist is to do this with permission – it has always been the purpose and function of the artist. I feel that I've been allowed to make whatever I like. What better way could there be to realise your fantasies?

RB You don't work in series but there are definite shifts that have occurred from period to period?

BW There have been shifts along the way, but there have also been recurring motifs. Feet, for instance, in *Negotiant* **1982** (p 85) and in particular the sole of the shoe. The hapless strolling woman in *Altruism and the law of diminishing returns* **1978** (pp 16-17), the sole of George's shoe used to strike a match in *The microbe as van Leuwenhoek may have seen it* **1977** (pp 72-73) and, latterly, the shoe as an unsuspecting means of transport in my film *Love story* **1996** (p 39). Who knows what this means? A lot of these things are completely unconscious. All artists have obsessions that come around again and again. The ability to see both sides, front and back, above and below, of anything at the same time is also a recurring theme. Even the cover image of this book allows both sides of a length of wire to be viewed at the same time.

RB You play with shifting points of view. Where is gravity coming from? Is it working from the top or from the bottom of the image?

BW I've always had a fascination with levels rising and falling, water tables and the like. I've been under the sea, into space, and inside the human body, figuratively speaking, of course. The spaces that are most interesting in the world aren't really attached to anything, they are floating just as the ideas that are most exciting are those which defy logical explanation. There are always components in these pictures which resonate and you can't say why. It is the defiance in this resonance that supplies the poetry.
I think a lot of the pieces which seem to defy gravity came about through the image in the camera being up-side-down. After years of seeing the sets up-side-

down and in reverse on the ground glass screen, I purchased a video camera and a monitor to see the image up the right way and in two dimensions. It didn't make much of a difference.

RB   Your work responds to issues in the real world. It is intense and serious and yet it has a powerful sense of humour, a dark humour.

BW   Artists are a product of their time. All art reflects the concerns of the day. Art history is ordinary history with a cultural slant. Look at any period of art history, it mimics, it relates, it reflects the historical events of the time and its cultural life.

RB   Sex issues? Sex and body functions?

BW   Sex has certainly been to the fore since the 1980s when the possibility of certain death erupted. I attempted to make colour alone deliver the emotive charge of the subject. Colours that were stressed, on fire, panicked, almost radioactive. Searing enough to cause breathlessness, not in a panting sexual sense but more akin to an ear-popping asthma attack or the effect of too much wasabi in a sushi bar.

RB   Colour is emotionally variable.

BW   In the early works the colour was rather non-descript, the colour of the New Zealand bush: flat grey-green, the colour of evergreens. The drabness of these artificial materials is the colour you get when you mix all colours together. The colour of underlay. The drabness was necessary to compound the air of gloom surrounding the desperate protagonists in pieces like *Guillemots* **1981** (p 166) and *One Bird* (p 19).

RB   Your work in the last decade has an obsession with bodily intersections between biology and technology. Internal organs or fluids moving inside the body, or outside the body, or fluids working within fluids.

BW   Biotechnology is the most exciting area of scientific inquiry at present; the areas of study are so mind-boglingly tiny, nano-engineering. (I love the prefix nano – it's a one thousand millionth of something.) It is the opposite to the endlessness of the cosmos. These two fields are intimately related even though in scale they couldn't be further apart. Forms visible through a microscope mimic those seen through a telescope. I find this wonderfully reassuring.

RB   Do you study scientific resources and astronomy?

BW   I love science, it's the root of everything. But basically I have no more than a layperson's knowledge of developments in astronomy and biology. My activity is mainly to marvel at whatever happens next. I have an urge to fabricate my own version of whatever it is. I think that it is in the half understood fabrication that the integrity of the amateur is manifest. By imagining it, you resolve making it with your own hands. It gives it a poetry and integrity that an image taken from a computer or the telescope wouldn't necessarily have. This integrity viewed in the right light is the nub of the work.

My first digitally-manipulated image *Asteroid and kidney stone* **1996** (pp 62-63) was made on a cinematic scale to accompany my film *Love Story*. It was assembled from several transparencies. One end of the image shows popcorn being sucked with great distortion into a black hole, of my own making in the depths of space. At the other end smaller, more jagged and scaly pieces of popcorn appear disporting themselves in what I imagine to be the interior of a human bladder.

RB   Your 1996 film *Love story* was commissioned?

BW   Yes, I was commissioned, along with nine others to create new work for 'Spellbound', an exhibition at the Hayward Gallery celebrating the centenary of cinema in London. I chose to make an animated film which celebrated the romance of both film and the venue. *Love Story* is a very cinematic sort of title. Half the films made are love stories. It seemed entirely suitable – at the end of the film the two lovers are taken off into space and that's the idea I extended with my piece *Asteroid and kidney stone*.

RB   Did you actually physically animate all the stop frames and make changes?

BW   No. I wrote and directed it. There was an animator, a cameraman and a prop person. It was shot on 35 mm stock and edited on Avid. The film was about popcorn. Anyone entering a cinema anywhere in the world is assailed by the aroma and detritus of popcorn. It is an unavoidable part of the cinema experience.

RB   Are you going to continue to work on a large scale?

BW   I don't know. It depends on the image; some images require a larger scale, others need a degree of intimacy. *Asteroid and kidney stone* was exceptional. In the past I have tried to make work on the scale of domestic doors, hoping the viewer could metaphorically walk into the picture, be sucked in and not notice the edges. What I have wanted all along is to make images that resonate with a universal appeal, that have the ability to move an audience without them being completely aware of it at the time. Realisation comes later as the reverberations continue and ring in the ears like a persistent mosquito. The image becomes fully memorable when the mosquito bites…

Breathe in...   *Breath*

WAK

In Maori legend the origin of Lake Wakatipu is accounted for by the destruction of a fearsome monster Te Tipua. Te Tipua was located fast asleep between the hills, made drowsy by the enervating north-west wind. As he slept, dry bracken and manuka were heaped on him and set alight. While still unconscious he involuntarily drew up his knees, so that the shape he assumed was that of the present lake. His head was at Glenorchy, his knees at Queenstown, and his feet at Kingston. The fire smouldered for days, and Te Tipua was consumed, except for his heart. The burning was responsible for the deep hole in the earth, in the midst of which his heart rested among the ashes. Water from the mountains filled the depression and covered the heart to a great depth; it still beats periodically with fierce activity to cause storms on the lake.

Normally, its quiet motion is said to cause the steady rise and fall of the lake's level, a phenomenon that all visitors can observe for themselves.

out... *Breathe in...*

TIPU

Strangely enough, the legend seems to have some bearing on early Pakeha reflections, for an article published in the *Otago Daily Times* in 1903 was entitled "The Heart-beats of Lake Wakatipu". This article drew attention to the phenomenon of the regular rise and fall in the lake level – something that occurs in only one other Otago lake. Since that date the rhythmic rise and fall in the level of the lake has been the subject of scientific investigation. In 1912 the *Canterbury Times* stated in an article that "the waters of the lake rise and fall three inches every five minutes with a pulsation similar to that of the human heart. No explanation of the phenomenon has ever been offered".

More recently the lake movement was investigated by the Science Society of the University of Otago, who reported that it was obviously seiche action, already well-known in lakes overseas, that produced oscillations in Lake Wakatipu. Their findings were published in Vol. 83 Part 4 (July, 1956) of the *Transactions of the Royal Society of New Zealand.*

Plates

Herbert Groves, an amateur lichenologist, has successfully developed and introduced a lichen (*Sponsio Grovesiaceae*) to the moist lining of his throat in order to become eligible for disability compensation. A keen punter he now studies form in earnest, investing sometimes to advantage, sometimes not.

Through skilful husbandry the lichen *Sponsio Grovesiaceae* has adapted successfully to the inclement environment of the human throat. Nutrients essential for this lichen's survival are filtered from the humid fug of despair, jubilation and nervous human effluvium peculiar to betting shops.

Herbert Groves
1973

As the living sap of a lobster is to the gourmet, so the condensation in the cap of a long distance swimmer is to the lobster.

The lobster
1976

Mrs Barnes' instinctive re-orientation un-equals her desire for self-advancement.

Mrs Barnes
1976

The microbe as
Van Leewenhoek
may have seen it
1977

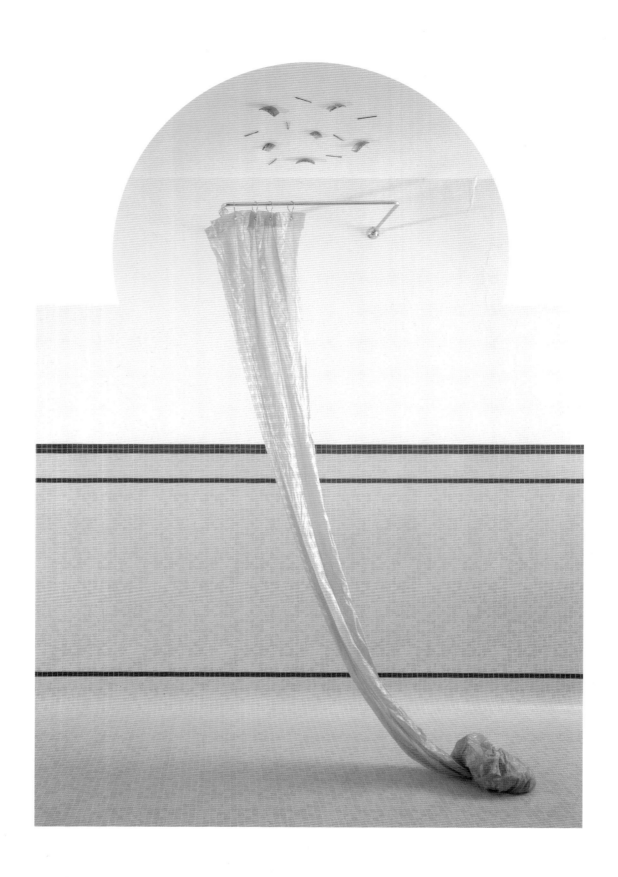

Untitled (pink curtain)
1979

The light and shade of expedience
1979

The mandatory second opinion
1978

Prehensile torpor
1977

The conservationist
1978

River crossing
1979

Chapped hands
1980

Escapist
1979

Shell shock
1983

Kiss
1982

Negotiant
1982

Abyssogramme
1983

Nemesis
1983

Autostrafe with handicap
1983

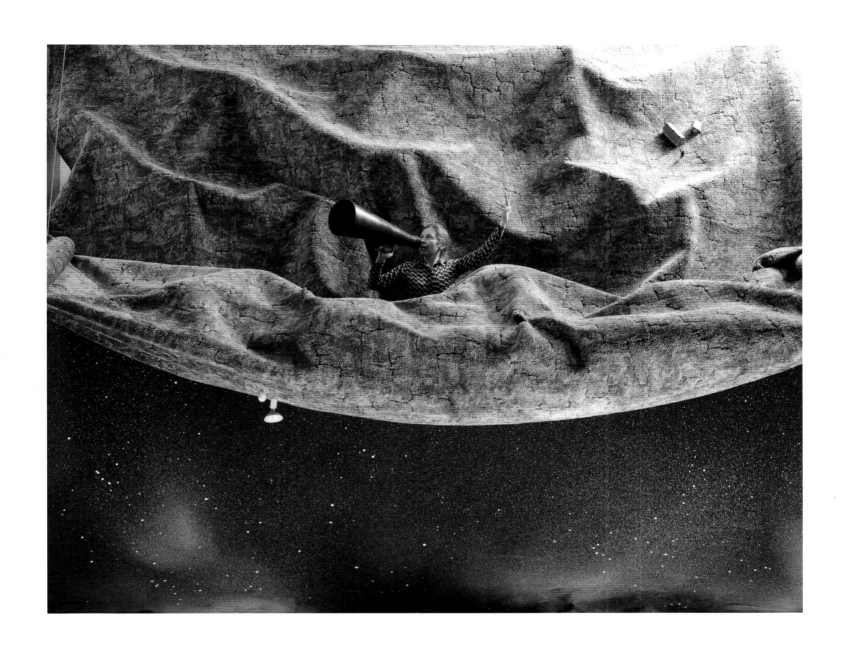

Supplicant
1984

Replenish
1984

Tortoise
1984

Renounce
1984

Strategist
1984

Sargasso
1984

Nourish
1984

Kibbutz
1985

Bedding
1985

Sphagnum
1985

Samurai
1985

Hyphen
1987

Tosser
1985

Cupid's sting
1986

Glorious morning
1986

Coppice
1986

Pupa rumba samba
1986

Medallion
1986

Enzyme
1986

Rudiments
1987

Coda
1987

Font
1987

First principles
1985

Truss
1987

Styrene
1988

Untitled
1987

Aurora and aspic
1988

Lagoon
1988

Undrained
1989

Darwin
1988

Beleaguer
1989

Plant
1989

Moth
1989

Croup
1989

Two views
1988

Chromosome
1989

Chattels
1989

Pillion and waiver
1988

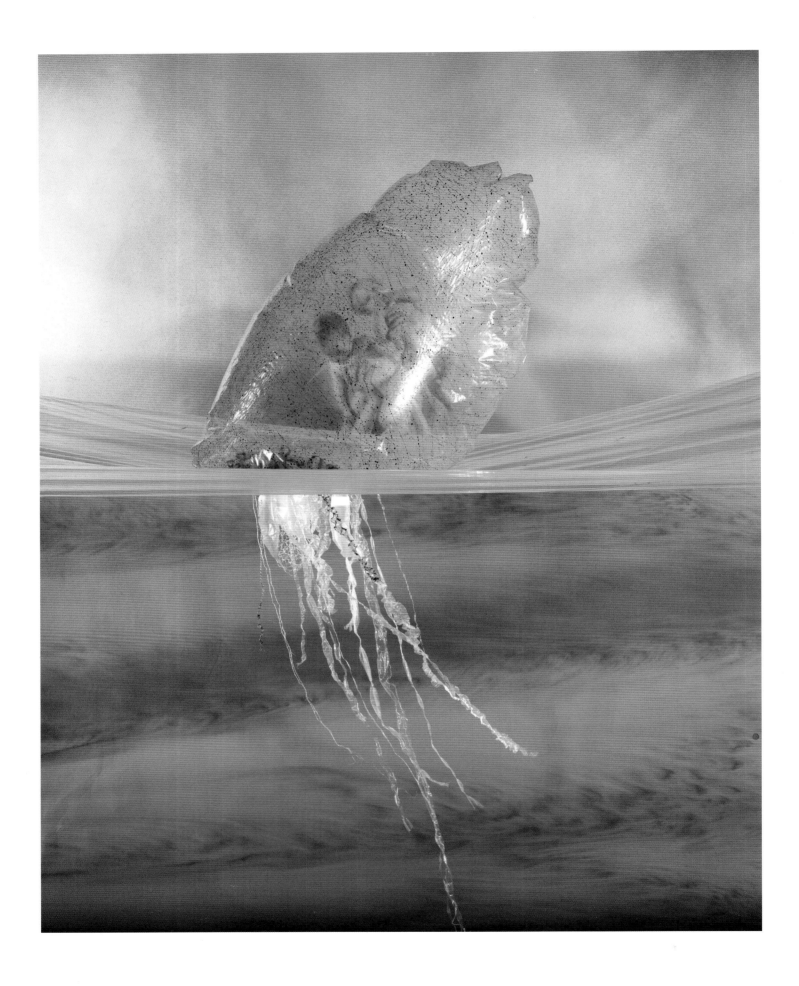

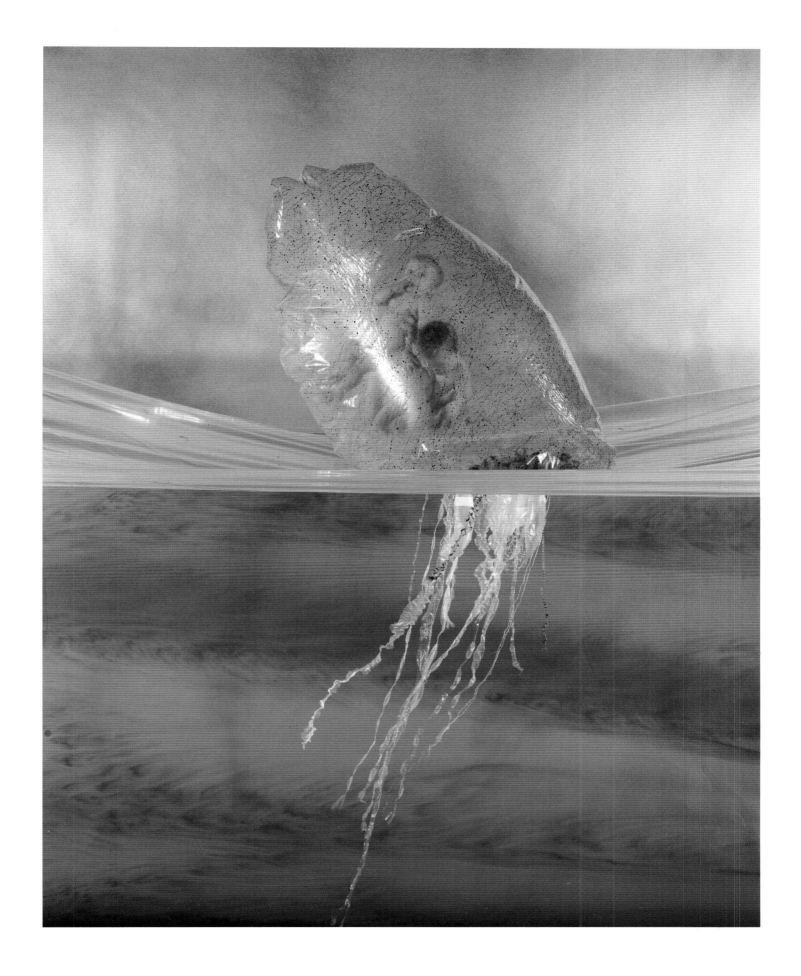

Suckling
1989

Mezzanine
1990

Atlas
1990

Sob
1993

Smother
1992

Sap
1993

Miasma & ampoule
1993

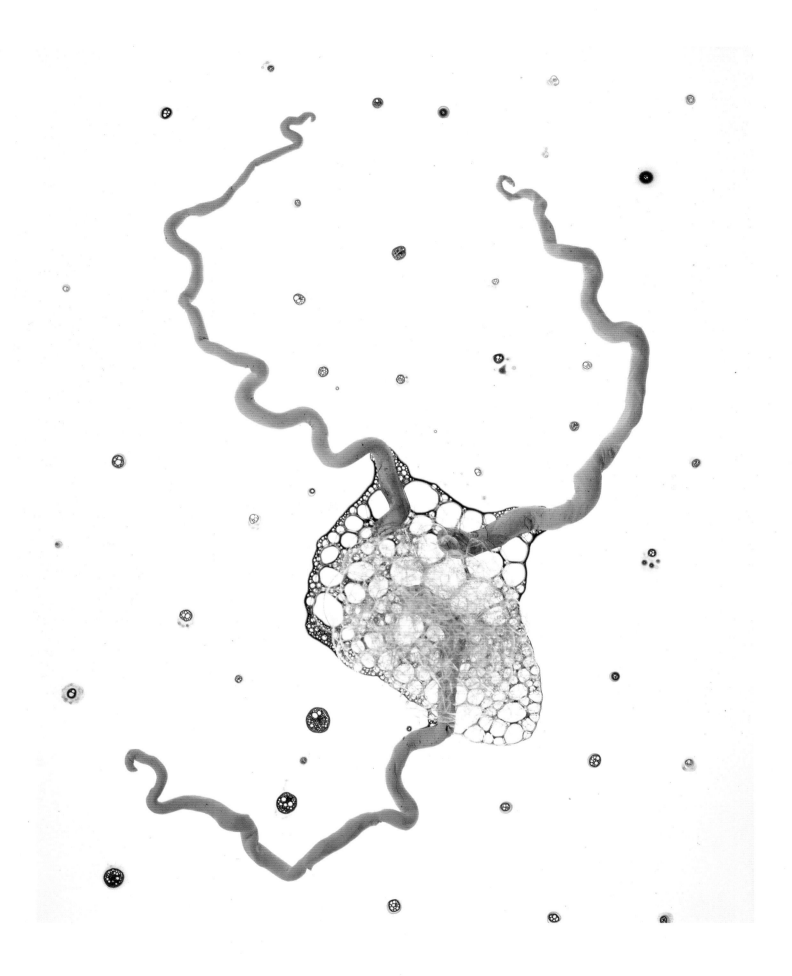

Zygote
1993

Stool
1993

Entomb
1993

Redoubt
1992

Tutelar
1993

Salvo
1993

Donor
1994

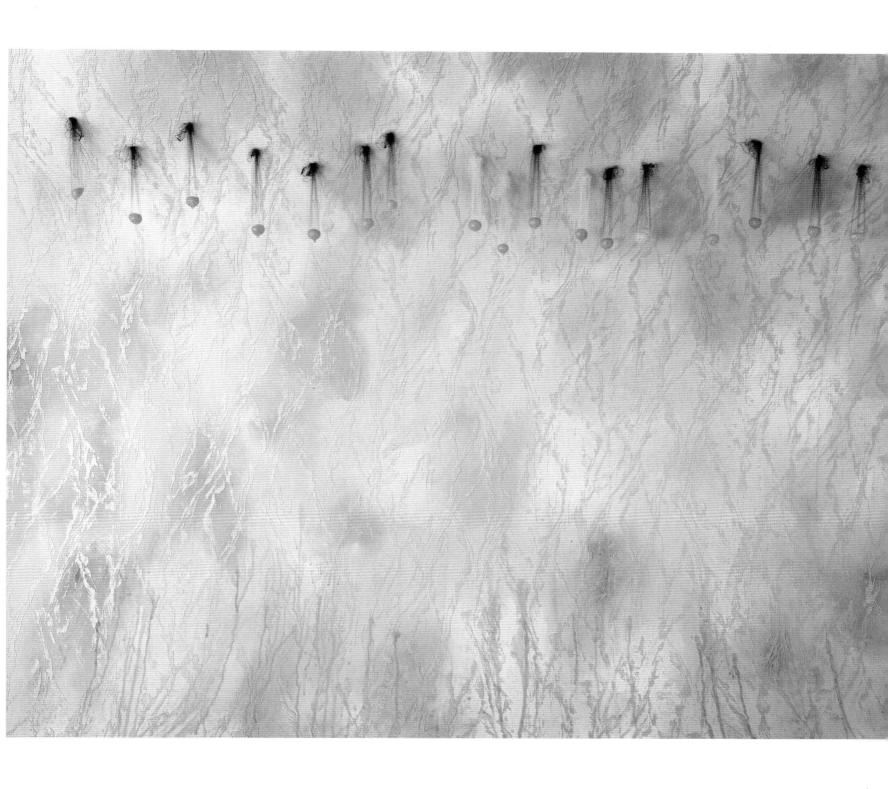

Ebb
1993

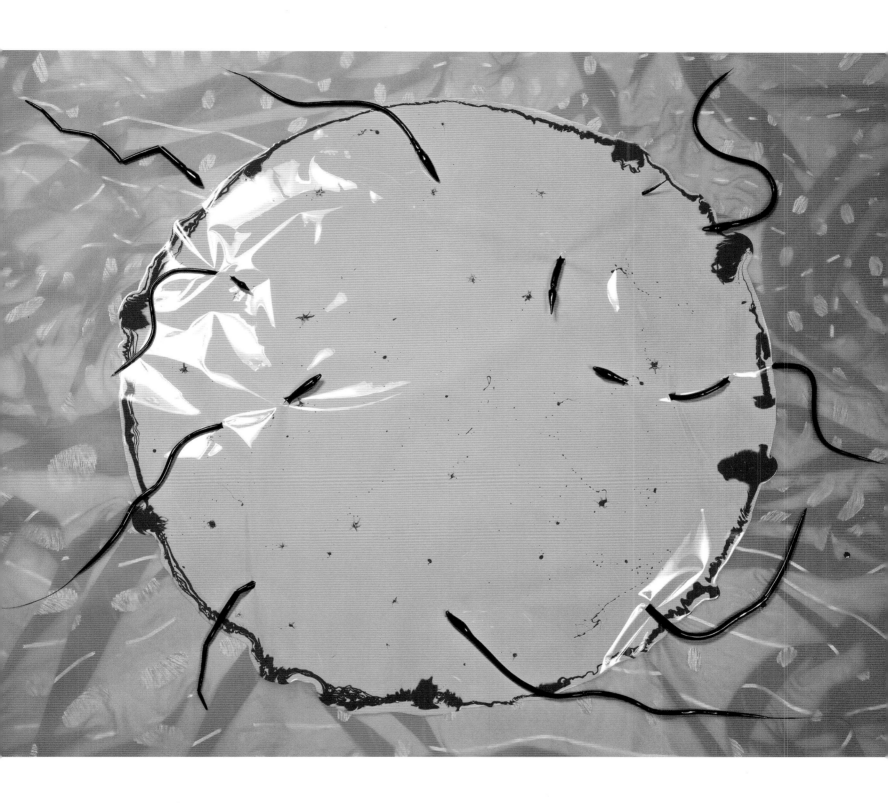

Corona
1994

Quorum
1996

Caucus
1994

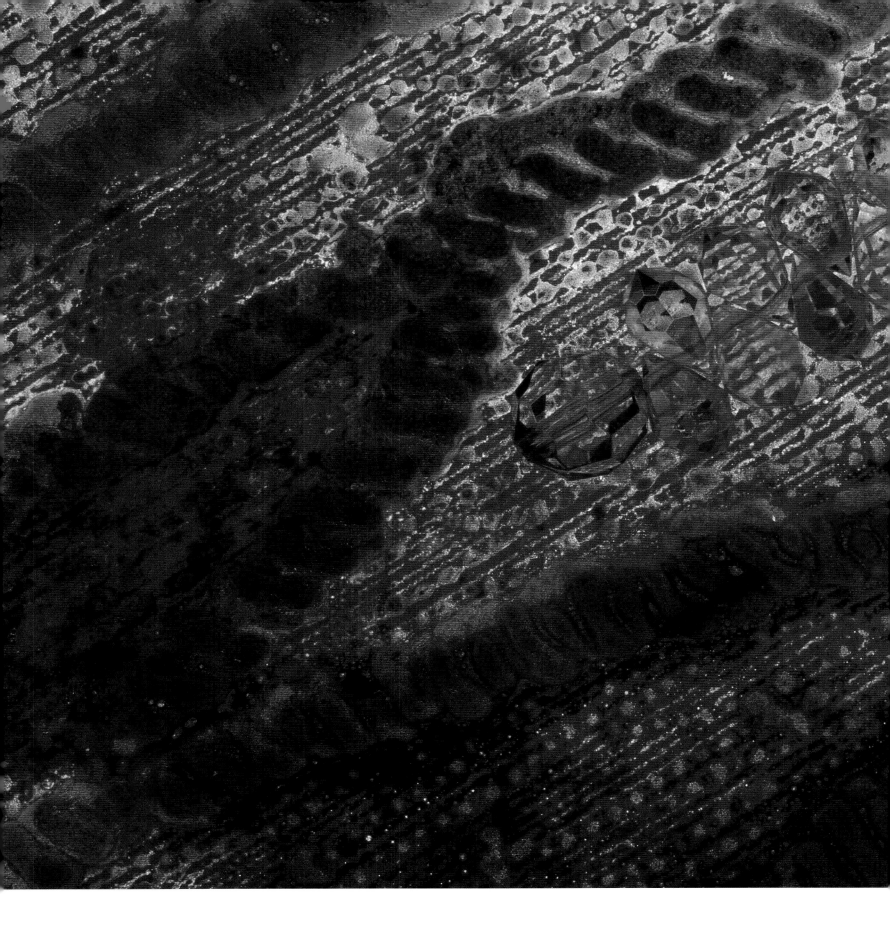

Vestige
1995

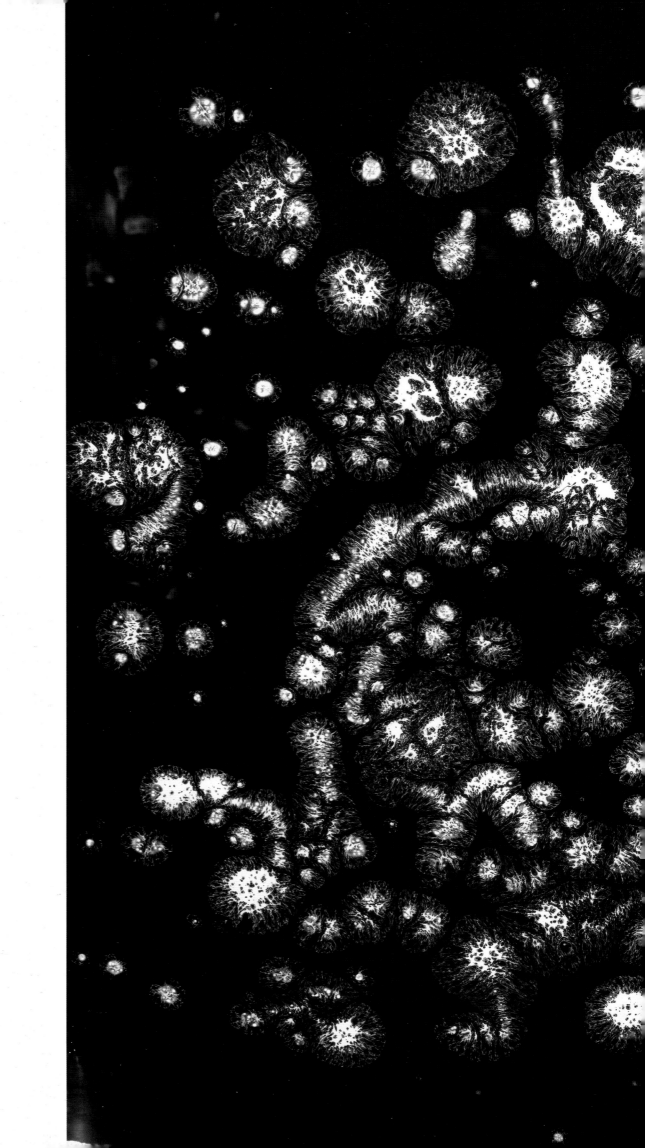

Tract
1995

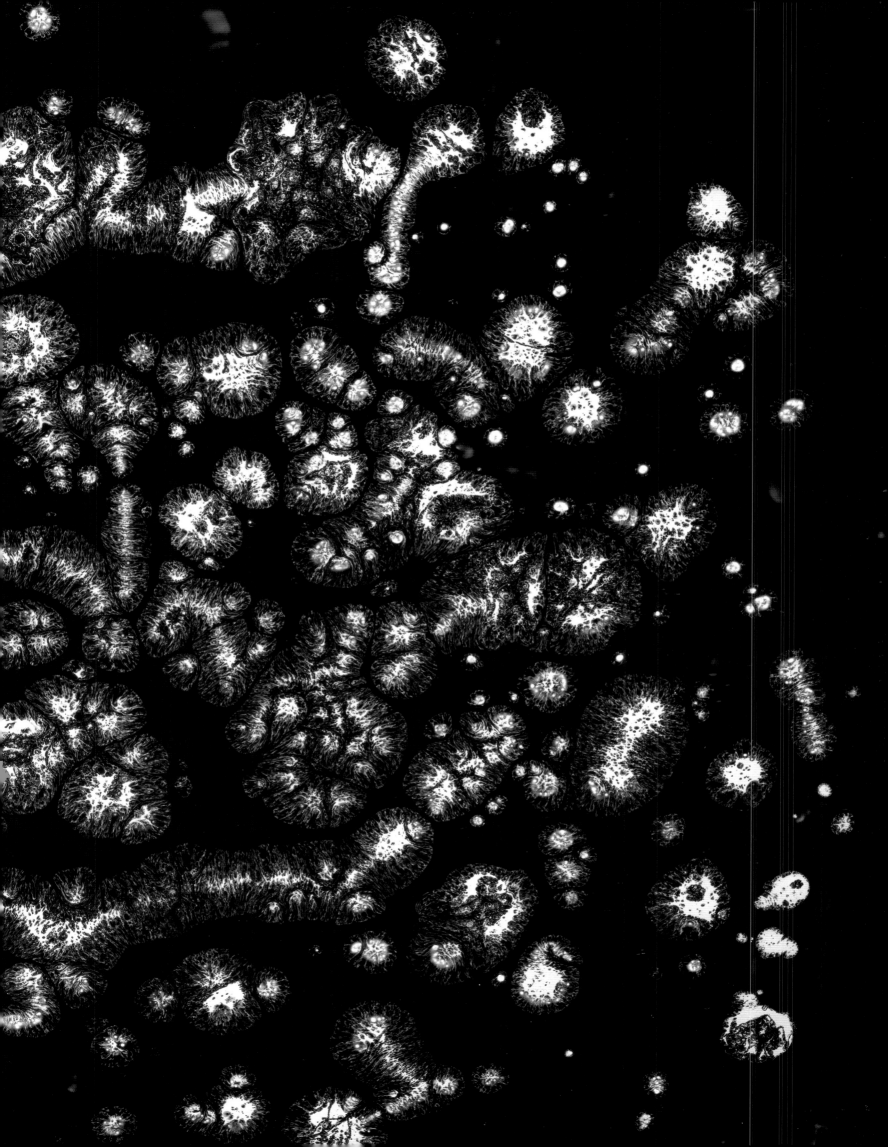

Nonage
1995

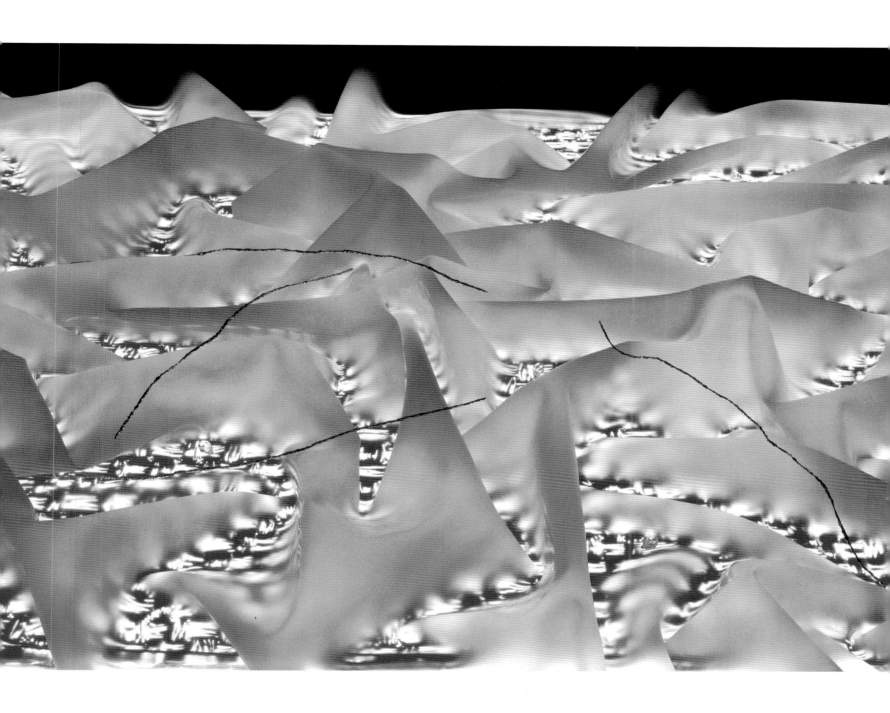

Terrain
1995

Villus
1996

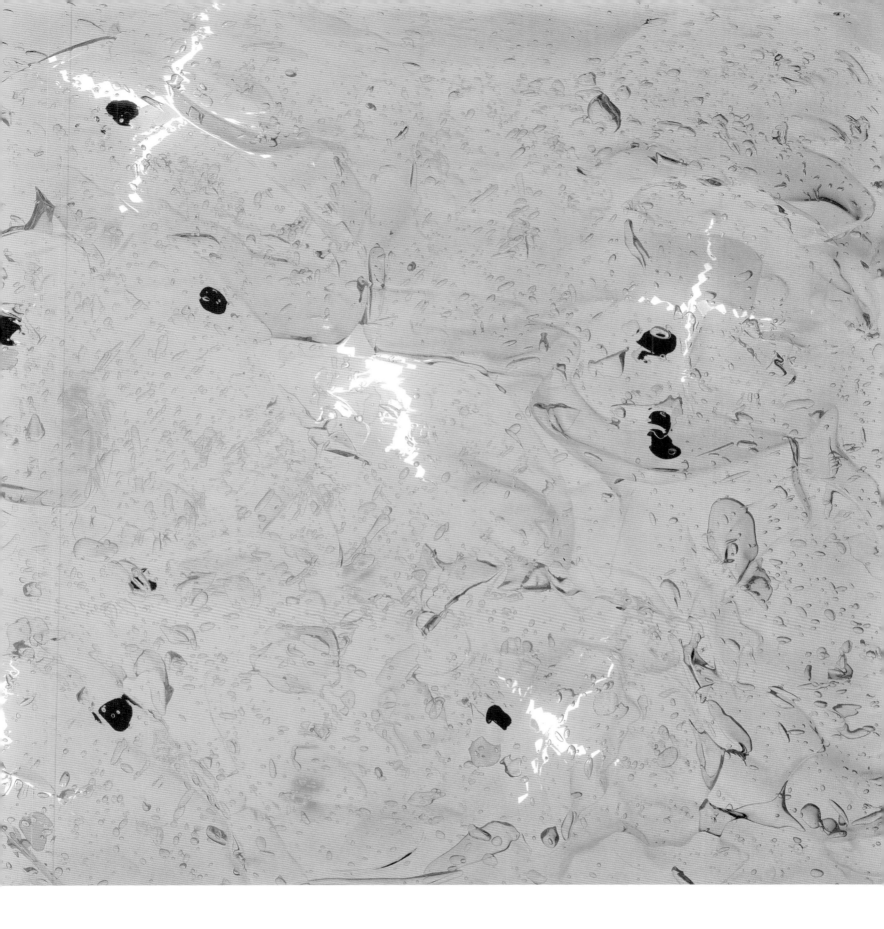

Retort
1996

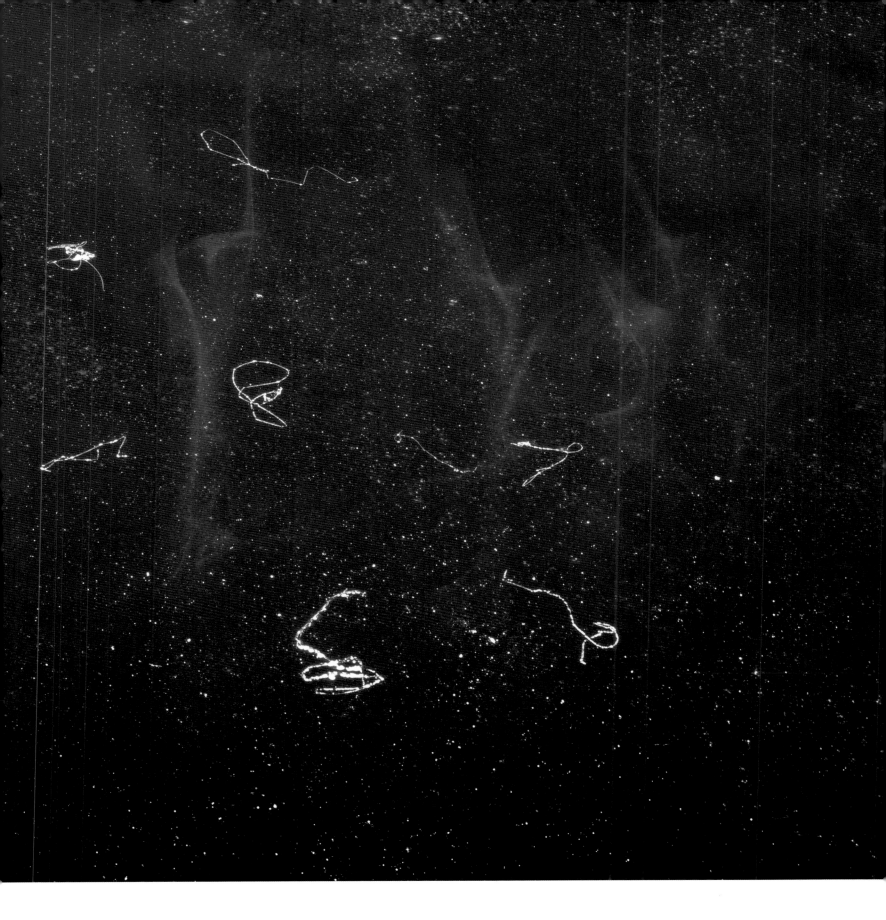

Agar and celeste
1996

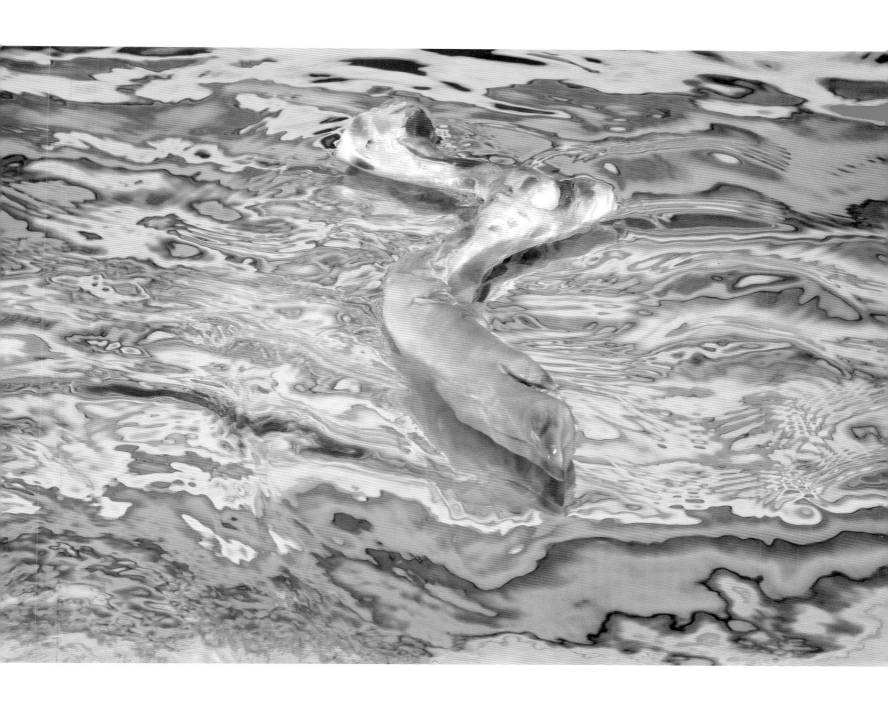

Unfrocked
1997

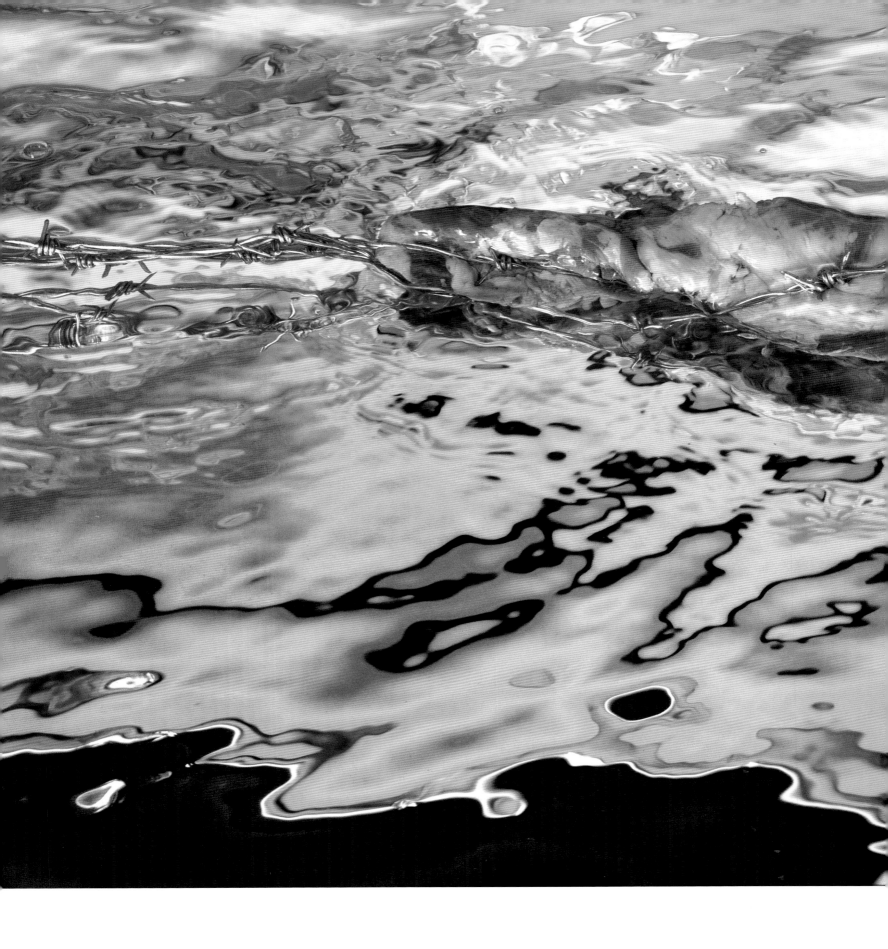

Wrack wring
1997

Guillemots
1981

Biography

1947   born Christchurch, New Zealand.

1968-71   studied at Canterbury University Department of Fine Arts, Christchurch

1972-75   studied at Royal College of Art, London

Lives and works in England.

Exhibition history

Solo exhibitions

All solo exhibitions are entitled 'Boyd Webb' unless otherwise indicated.

1976   London: Robert Self Gallery (travelled to Newcastle: PMJ Self Gallery).

1977   Sheffield: Graves Art Gallery.
Newcastle: Robert Self Gallery.
Edinburgh: Graeme Murray Gallery.

1978   Hartlepool: Gray Art Gallery and Museum.
Düsseldorf: Konrad Fischer Gallery.
Athens: Jean and Karen Bernier Gallery.
Bristol: Arnolfini Art Gallery (travelled to Cardiff: Chapter Arts Centre).
London: Whitechapel Art Gallery.

1979   Edinburgh: New Belfast: Arts Council Gallery.
New York: Sonnabend Gallery.
Paris: Galerie Sonnabend.

1980   Rotterdam: Galerie 't Venster. 'Boyd Webb fotowerken'.
Krefeld: Museum Haus Lange. 'Boyd Webb – Norbet Woolf'.

1981   Geneva: Galerie Loyse Oppenheim.
London: Anthony d'Offay Gallery.
Southampton: John Hansard Gallery.
Auckland: Auckland City Art Gallery (travelled to venues throughout NZ, including
    Wellington: National Art Gallery).
New York: Sonnabend Gallery.

1982   Karlsruhe: Badischer Kunstverein (travelled to Münster: Westfälischer Kunstverein).
Athens: Jean and Karen Bernier Gallery.

1983   Paris: Musée National d'Art Moderne, Centre Georges Pompidou.
Paris: Galerie Crousel-Hussenot.
Eindhoven: Stedelijk van Abbemuseum (travelled to Bern: Kunsthalle; Lyon: Le Nouveau
    Musée; Leeds City Art Gallery; La Roche-sur-Yon: Musée Municipal).

1984   London: Anthony d'Offay Gallery.

1985   Chicago: Northern Illinois University (travelled to Amherst: University of Massachusetts;
    Knoxville: University of Tennessee; Long Beach: University Art Museum, California State
    University).
New York: Sonnabend Gallery.

1986   Adelaide: Adelaide Festival of the Arts (travelled to Melbourne: Australian Centre for
           Contemporary Art; Tasmania: Centre for the Arts, University of Tasmania; Sydney: Power
           Gallery of Contemporary Art, University of Sydney).
           Auckland: Sue Crockford Gallery.

1987   Athens: Jean Bernier Gallery.
           Lisbon: Galeria Cómicos.
           London: Whitechapel Art Gallery. 'Boyd Webb: photographs 1981-1987' (travelled to
           Hanover: Kestner-Gesellschaft; Edinburgh: The Fruitmarket Gallery; Los Angeles: Museum
           of Contemporary Art).

1988   Santa Monica: Meyers/Bloom Gallery.

1989   London: Anthony d'Offay Gallery.
           Manchester: Cornerhouse.
           Munich: Galerie Bernd Klüser.
           Paris: Galerie Ghislaine Hussenot.
           New York: Sonnabend Gallery.

1990   Athens: Jean Bernier Gallery.
           Limoges: FRAC du Limousin. 'Boyd Webb, œuvres-works: 1988-90'.
           Santa Monica: Meyers-Bloom Gallery.
           Washington, DC: Hirshhorn Museum and Sculpture Garden. 'Directions – Boyd Webb'.

1991   Paris: Espace d'art contemporain, OCO. 'Boyd Webb 1973-1979'.

1992   Kansas: Johnson County Community College Gallery of Art. 'Boyd Webb: Photographs
           1988-89'.
           Santa Monica: Meyers-Bloom Gallery.

1993   Coimbra: Encontros de Photografia. 'Caldera' installation.
           Geneva: Centre d'Art Contemporain.
           Paris: Galerie Ghislaine Hussenot.

1994   British Council. VIII Indian Triennale exhibition (travelled to New Delhi: Lalit Kala Akademi;
           Calcutta: Birla Academy of Art and Culture; Madras: Lalit Kala Akademi Gallery;
           Bangalore: Karnataka Chitrakala Parishath; Ahmedabad: Ravishankar Raval Art Gallery;
           Hong Kong: The Hong Kong Arts Centre; Antwerp: Museum van Hedendaagse Kunst.
           Larger version concurrently travelled to Preston: Harris Museum and Art Gallery;
           Brighton Museum and Art Gallery; Glasgow: Centre for Contemporary Arts;
           Birmingham: Ikon Gallery; Derry: Orchard Gallery).
           Santa Monica: Ruth Bloom Gallery.

1995   New York: Sonnabend Gallery. 'Boyd Webb: new work'.

1996   Nice, France: Villa Arson. 'Septembre de la Photo'.

1997   Auckland: Auckland Art Gallery (travelling to Northland: Whangarei Art Museum;
           Palmerston North: Manawatu Art Gallery; Hamilton: Waikato Museum of Art and
           History; Wellington: City Gallery; New Plymouth: Govett-Brewster Art Gallery;

Wanganui: Sargeant Art Gallery; Rotorua: Museum of Art and History; Nelson: Bishop
Suter Art Gallery; Masterton; Wairarapa Arts Centre; Christchurch: Robert McDougall Art
Gallery; tour continuing).
Auckland: Sue Crockford Gallery.
London: Anthony d'Offay Gallery.
Nancy: Galerie Robert Doisneau.
New York: Tanya Bonakdar Gallery. 'Boyd Webb: early work'.
Rouen: Grande Galerie – Aitre Saint-Maclou.

Group exhibitions

1970   Christchurch: CSA. '4 artists'.

1971   Christchurch: CSA. '4 sculptors' (travelled to Wellington: NZ Display Centre, 1972)
Christchurch. 'Sculpture on the Avon river'.
Christchurch: Robert McDougall Art Gallery. '30 plus'.
Auckland: Auckland City Art Gallery. 'New Zealand young contemporaries'.

1973   London: New Zealand House, Haymarket. 'Six New Zealand artists' (travelled to Auckland:
Auckland City Art Gallery, 1974).

1975   London: Robert Self Gallery.

1976   Auckland: Auckland City Art Gallery. 'Pan Pacific biennale'.

1977   Graz: Künstlerhaus. 'Time, words and the camera: photoworks by British artists'
(travelled to Innsbruck: Galerie im Taxipalais; Vienna: Künstlerhaus; Bochum: Museum
Bochum).

1979   Stuttgart. 'Europa '79'.
Zürich: InK, Halle für internationale neue Kunst. 'With a certain smile'.

1980   Arts Council of Great Britain. 'About 70 photographs' (touring exhibition).
British Council. 'Photography and the medium' (travelled to Norway, Poland, Yugoslavia,
The Netherlands, Denmark, Spain).
London: Lisson Gallery.
New York: Sonnabend Gallery.
Santa Barbara: University of California. 'Invented images' (travelled to Portland Art
Museum; Santa Cruz: Mary Porter Sesnon Art Gallery, University of California).
Sheffield: Mappin Art Gallery. 'Artist and camera' (travelled to Sunderland Art Gallery;
Liverpool: Open Eye Gallery and School of Architecture; Llandudno: Mostyn Art Gallery;
Southampton: Southampton Art Gallery and John Hansard Gallery; Bristol: Arnolfini Gallery;
London: Institute of Contemporary Arts).

1981   Bonn: Rheinisches Landesmuseum. 'Das Porträt in der Fotografie.'
Dayton, Ohio: Wright State University. 'Fabricated to be photographed' (travelled to
New York: PS 1).
Edinburgh: Fruitmarket Gallery. 'New works of contemporary art and music'.
Glasgow: Third Eye Centre. 'Art and the sea' (travelled to Sheffield: Mappin Art Gallery;

Stoke: Stoke City Art Gallery; Durham: DLI Museum and Arts Centre; Bradford:
   Cartwright Hall).
New York: Sidney Janis Gallery. 'New directions'.
New York: Sonnabend Gallery.
London: Anthony d'Offay Gallery.
Paris: Galerie Chantel Crousel.
Syracuse, New York: Everson Museum of Art and International Center for Photography,
New York. 'The new color'.
Vienna: Neue Sezession. 'Erweiterte Fotografie'.

1982   Rotterdam: Lijnbaan Centrum. 'Staged photo events'.
        Sydney: Art Gallery of New South Wales. 'Vision in disbelief' (4th biennale of Sydney
           exhibition).
        Kassel. 'documenta 7'.

1983   London: Anthony d'Offay Gallery. 'Works on paper'.
        London: Hayward Gallery. 'The sculpture show: fifty sculptors at the Serpentine and the
           South Bank'.
        Paris: Musée National d'Art Moderne, Centre Georges Pompidou. 'Images fabriquées'.

1984   Cadillac-Gironde: Château des ducs d'Epernon. 'Histoires de sculpture'.
        California: Laguna Beach Museum of Art. 'Anxious interiors'.
        London: Arts Council of Great Britain. 'The British art show: old allegiances and new
           directions, 1979-1984' (travelled to Birmingham: City of Birmingham Museum and Art
           Gallery and Ikon Gallery; Edinburgh: Royal Scottish Academy; Sheffield: Mappin Art
           Gallery; Southampton Art Gallery).

1985   Bern: Kunsthalle. 'Alles und noch viel mehr: das poetische ABC'.
        Humlebaek, Denmark: Louisiana Museum. 'Sculpture: 9 artists from England'.
        Leeds: Leeds City Art Gallery. 'The irresistible object: still life 1600-1985'.
        London: Tate Gallery. 'Forty years of modern art 1945-1985'.
        Lyon: Le Nouveau Musée. 'Collection souvenir'.
        New York: Queens Museum. 'The real big picture'.
        Paris: Musée National d'Art Moderne, Centre Georges Pompidou. 'Atelier Polaroid'.
        Paris: Grande Halle de la Gillette. 'Nouvelle biennale de Paris'.
        Southampton: John Hansard Gallery, University of Southampton. 'L'indifférent'.
        Venice: Venice Biennale. 'Aperto'.

1986   Cardiff: Ffotogallery. 'True stories and photofictions' (travelled to Hull: Posterngate Gallery).
        Frankfurt: Frankfurter Kunstverein and Schirn Kunsthalle. 'Prospect '86'.
        London: Photographers' Gallery. 'Photography as performance'.
        Minneapolis: Walker Art Center. 'Sculpture into photography' (travelled to Chicago:
           Museum of Contemporary Art).
        Montreal: Musée d'Art Contemporain. 'La magie de l'image'.
        New York: White columns. 'Signs of the real'.
        Swansea: Glynn Vivian Art Gallery. 'Contrariwise: surrealism and Britain 1930-1986'
           (travelled to Bath: Victoria Art Centre; Newcastle: Polytechnic Gallery; Llandudno:
           Moyston Art Gallery).

1987   British Council. 'Inscriptions and inventions: British photography in the 1980s' (travelled to
           Belgium; Luxembourg; Italy).

Darlington: Arts Centre. 'Conversations'.

London: Anthony d'Offay Gallery. 'About sculpture'.

London: Photographers' Gallery and Cardiff: Ffotogallery. 'Mysterious coincidences' (travelled to California: Long Beach Museum; Hong Kong Art Centre; Melbourne: ACCA; Hamilton: Waikato Museum of Art and History).

Minneapolis: Walker Art Center. 'Cross-references: sculpture into photography' (travelled to Chicago: Museum of Contemporary Art, 1988).

Stuttgart: Württembergischer Kunstverein. 'Zeitgeschichte' (travelled to Berlin: Haus am Waldsee; Hamburg: Kunstverein; Frankfurter Kunstverein; Lucerne: Kunstmuseum; Bonn: Rheinisches Landesmuseum).

1988 Auckland: Auckland City Art Gallery. 'NZXI' (travelled to Sydney: Art Gallery of New South Wales; Brisbane: Museum of Contemporary Art).

Bruxelles: Musées Royaux des Beaux-Arts de Belgique. 'Viewpoint: British art of the 1980s'.

Nantes: Musée des Beaux-Arts. 'Matter of facts, Photographie: art contemporain en Grand-Bretagne' (travelled to St Etienne: Le Musée d'Art Moderne; Caves Sainte-Croix: Metz pour la Photographie).

Nottingham: Nottingham Castle Museum. 'Inside/Outside'.

Stoke-on-Trent: City Museum and Art Gallery. 'Object and image: aspects of British art in the 1980s'.

Zürich: Museum für Gestaltung. 'Britische Sicht! Fotografie aus England'.

1989 Houston: Museum of Fine Arts. 'The art of photography 1839-1989' (travelled to Canberra: Australian National Gallery; London: Royal Academy).

London: Barbican Art Centre. 'Through the looking glass'.

Ludwigshafen: BASF Feierabendhaus. 'Lebenslinien: vier Künstler aus Großbritannien' (travelled to Liverpool: Tate Gallery).

Munich: Kunstverein. 'Das konstruierte Bild' (travelled to Nürnberg: Kunsthalle; Bremen: Forum Böttcherstrasse; Karlsruhe: Badischer Kunstverein).

Paris: Musée National d'Art Moderne, Centre Georges Pompidou. 'L'invention d'un art'.

Tokyo: INFAS. 'Seven artists 89'.

York: Impressions Gallery. 'The globe'.

1990 Barcelona: Centre d'Art Contemporani Santa Monica. 'To be and not to be'.

Bath: Beaux Arts. 'Tribute to Peter Fuller'.

Liverpool: Tate Gallery. 'Lifelines – four British artists'.

London: The Showroom. 'UK → USSR' (travelled to Kiev: House of the Artist; Moscow: Central House of the Artist).

Sydney: Art Gallery of New South Wales. 'The readymade boomerang: certain relations in 20th century art' (8th biennale of Sydney exhibition).

Tokyo: Setagaya Museum. 'British art now: a subjective view' (travelled to Fukuoka Art Museum; Nagoya City Art Museum; Tochigi Prefectural Museum of Fine Arts; Hyogo Prefectural Museum of Modern Art; Hiroshima City Museum of Contemporary Art).

Vienna: Vienna Festival. 'Von der Natur in der Kunst'.

1991 Bergen: Project Contemporary Art. 'Blind navigator – the heritage of surrealism'.

London: British Council. 'De composition: constructed photography in Britain' (toured to South America, including Mexico).

Manchester: City Art Gallery. 'Modern painter: a memorial exhibition for Peter Fuller'.

Wrøclaw: Museum of Architecture. 'New spaces of architecture'.

1992   London: Hayward Gallery. 'Doubletake: collective memory & current art' (travelled to
                  Vienna: Kunsthalle).

1993   Caen, France: Centre d'histoire de l'art contemporain. 'C'est pas la fin du monde'.

1994   Kent: Herbert Read Gallery. 'Crossroads' (travelled to Ipswich: Wolsey Art Gallery; Bruxelles:
             Centre d'Art Contemporain; Caen: FRAC de Basse Normandie; Stoke-on-Trent: City
                  Museum and Art Gallery).
             London: Saatchi Gallery. 'A positive view'.
             London: Anthony d'Offay Gallery. 'Sculpture'.
             New Plymouth: Govett-Brewster Art Gallery. 'Power works: from the MCA collection'
                  (travelled to Wellington: National Art Gallery; Sydney: MCA).
             St Petersburg: Russian Museum. 'A changing world: fifty years of sculpture from the British
                  Council collection' (travelled to Moscow: Pushkin Museum).
             Seoul, Korea: Seoul 600 International Art Festival. 'Humanism and technology: The human
                  figure in industrial society'.

1995   Austria: Kunsthalle Krems. 'Wasser und Wein: zwei Dinge des Lebens'.
             Dallas: The McKinney Avenue Contemporary. 'Dare'.

1996   Cahors: Photographie & Arts Visuels. 'Le printemps de Cahors '96'. (travelled to
                  Copenhagen: Portalen Contemporary Art Centre).
             Frankfurt: Frankfurter Kunstverein. 'Prospect '96'.
             London: Hayward Gallery. 'Spellbound: art and film'.
             Nice: Centre Municipal de la Photographie. 'Septembre de la photo 96'.

1997   Auckland: Artspace. 'alt.nature'.
             Berlin: Neue Gesellschaft für Bildende Kunst. 'Contemporary British photography' (travelled
                  to Ludwigshafen: Kunstverein).
             London: Purdy Hicks Gallery. 'A cloudburst of material possessions: A fantasy on a drawing
                  by Leonardo da Vinci' (travelled to Eastbourne: Towner Art Gallery and Museum;
                  Worcester: City Art Gallery and Museum; Mead: Gallery Coventry).
             Ridgefield, Connecticut: The Aldrich Museum of Contemporary Art. 'Making it real'
                  (travelled to Iceland: Reykjavik Municipal Art Museum; Portland, Maine: Portland
                  Museum of Art; Charlottesville: Bayly Art Museum, University of Virginia).

Bibliography

Solo exhibition catalogues

1978   London: Robert Self Gallery. *Tableaux* (introduction by Stuart Morgan).
London: Whitechapel Art Gallery. *Boyd Webb* (introduction, 'Contrary illuminations', by Nicholas Serota).

1980   Krefeld: Museum Haus Lange. *Boyd Webb – Norbert Woolf* (essay by Marianna Stockebrand).

1981   Auckland: Auckland City Art Gallery. *Boyd Webb, photographic works 1976-1981* (introduction by Hamish Keith).

1982   Karlsruhe: Badischer Kunstverein. *Boyd Webb: Photoskulpturen* (essay by Michael Schwarz; catalogue insert, 'A twist in the tail: Boyd Webb and the directorial tradition', by John Roberts).

1983   Eindhoven: Stedelijk Van Abbemuseum. *Boyd Webb* (essay, 'Losing your bearings: Boyd Webb', by Bernard Blistène; extracts from a conversation between Jan Debbaut and Jean-Hubert Martin).

1986   Adelaide: Festival of the Arts. *Boyd Webb* (essay, 'Boyd Webb,' by Richard Cork).

1987   London: Whitechapel Art Gallery. *Boyd Webb: photographs 1981-87* (essay, 'Global strategies', by Stuart Morgan).

1990   Limousin: Fonds Regional d'Art Contemporain. *Boyd Webb, œuvres – works: 1988-90* (essay, 'Un objet *secondaire*, un objet désolé/The *secondary* object, a desolate object', by Frédérick Paul).
Washington, DC: Hirshhorn Museum and Sculpture Garden. *Directions, Boyd Webb* (essay by Sidney Lawrence).

1991   Paris: Espace d'art contemporain, OCO. *Boyd Webb 1973-1979* (essay, 'Vingt ans après...', by Frédérick Paul).

1992   Kansas: Johnson Community College & Gallery of Art. *Boyd Webb: photographs 1988-89* (abridged essay by Sidney Lawrence).

1994   London: British Council. *Boyd Webb* (introduction by Andrea Rose; essay, 'A degree of unease', by Greg Hilty).

Group exhibition catalogues

1971   Auckland: Auckland City Art Gallery. *Young contemporaries.*

1976   Graz: Neue Galerie am Landesmuseum Johanneum. *Time, words and the camera: photoworks by British artists.*

1979   Stuttgart: 'Europa '79'. Special issue, *Kunstforum.* vol 36, no 6.
Zürich: InK, Halle für Internationale Neue Kunst. *With a certain smile.*

1980   London: Arts Council of Great Britain. *About 70 photographs.*
London: Arts Council of Great Britain. *Artist and camera.*
Santa Barbara, CA: University of California Art Museum. *Invented images.*

1981   Bonn: Rheinisches Landesmuseum. *Das Porträt in der Fotografie.*
Dayton, Ohio: Wright State University. *Fabricated to be photographed.*
Edinburgh: Graeme Murray Gallery. *New works of contemporary art and music.*
Vienna: Neue Secession. *Erweiterte Fotografie* (5th international biennale exhibition catalogue).

1982   London: Institute of Contemporary Arts. *Art and the sea.*
Kassel: Verlag Paul Dierichs & Co. *documenta 7.*
Sydney: Biennale of Sydney. *Vision in disbelief* (4th biennale of Sydney exhibition catalogue).

1983   London: Arts Council of Great Britain. *The sculpture show: fifty sculptors at the Serpentine and the South Bank.*
Paris: Musée National d'Art Moderne, Centre Georges Pompidou. *Images fabriquées.*

1984   Cadillac-Gironde: Château des ducs d'Epernon. *Histoires de sculpture.*
California: Laguna Beach Museum of Art. *Anxious interiors: an exhibition of tableaux photography and sculpture.*
London: Orbis/Arts Council of Great Britain. *The British art show: old allegiances and new directions, 1979-1984.*

1985   Bern: Benteli. *Alles und noch viel mehr: das poetische ABC.*
Humlebaek: Louisiana Museum. *Sculpture: 9 artists from England.*
Leeds: Leeds City Art Galleries. *The irresistible object: still life, 1600-1985.*
London: Tate Gallery. *Forty years of modern art 1945-1985.*
Paris: Electa Moniteur. *Nouvelle biennale de Paris* (13th biennale of Paris exhibition catalogue).
Paris: Centre Georges Pompidou. *Atelier polaroid.*
Southampton: John Hansard Gallery, University of Southampton. *L'indifférent.*
Venice: Venice Biennale. *Aperto.*

1986   Cardiff: Ffotogallery. *True stories and photofictions.*
Frankfurt: Frankfurter Kunstverein and Kunsthalle Schirn. *Prospect 86: eine internationale Ausstellung aktueller Kunst.*
London: Photographers Gallery. *Photography as performance.*
Minneapolis: Walker Art Center. *Cross references: sculpture into photography.*
Montreal: Musée d'Art Contemporain. *La magie de l'image.*
Swansea: Glynn Vivian Art Gallery. *Contrariwise: surrealism and Britain, 1930-1986.*

1987   London: Arts Council of Great Britain. *Conversations.*
London: British Council. *Inscriptions and inventions: British photography in the 1980s.*
London: Anthony d'Offay Gallery. *About sculpture.*
London: Photographers' Gallery. *Mysterious coincidences.*
Minneapolis: Walker Art Centre. *Cross-references: sculpture into photography.*
Stuttgart: Württembergischer Kunstverein. *Zeitgeschichte.*

1988   Auckland: Auckland City Art Gallery. *NZ XI* (essay by Francis Pound).
Brussels: Musée Royaux des Beaux-Arts de Bélgique. *Viewpoint: British art of the 1980s.*
Nantes: Musée des Beaux-Arts. *Photographie: art contemporain en Grande-Bretagne.*
Zürich: Museum für Gestaltung. *Britische Sicht! Fotografie aus England.*

1989   Bristol: Watershed Media Centre. *From object to image: photo sculpture.*
New Haven: Yale University Press. *The art of photography 1839-1989.*
London: Barbican Art Centre. *Through the looking glass: photographic art in Britain 1945-1989.*
Ludwigshafen: BASF Aktiengesellschaft. *Lebenslinien: vier künstler aus Großbritannien.*
Paris: Centre National de la Photographie. *De la photographie comme un des beaux-arts.*
Paris: Centre Georges Pompidou. *L'invention d'un art: cent-cinquantième anniversaire de la photographie.*
Tokyo: INFAS. *Seven artists '89.*
York: Impressions Gallery. *The globe.*
Zurich: Édition Stemmle. *Constructed realities: the art of staged photography.*

1990   Barcelona: Centre d'Art Contemporani Santa Monica. *To be and not to be.*
Bath: Beaux Arts. *Tribute to Peter Fuller.*
Liverpool: Tate Gallery Liverpool. *Lifelines: four British artists.*
Sydney: Biennale of Sydney. *The readymade boomerang: certain relations in 20th century art* (8th biennale of Sydney exhibition catalogue).
Tokyo: Asahi Shimbun. *British art now: a subjective view.*
Vienna: Vienna Festival. *Von der Natur in der Kunst: eine Ausstellung der Wiener Festwochen.*

1991   Bergen: Project Contemporary Art. *Blind navigator – the heritage of surrealism.*
London: British Council. *Decomposition: constructed photography in Britain.*
Manchester: City Art Gallery. *Modern painter: a memorial exhibition for Peter Fuller.*

1992   Caujolle, Christian, *Variations gitanes.* Paris: Flammarion.
London: Hayward Gallery. *Double take: collective memory & current art* (essay by Lynne Cooke).
Rennes: Centre d'Histoire de l'Art Contemporain. *C'est pas la fin du monde: un point de vue sur l'art des années 80.*

1994   London: British Council. *A changing world: fifty years of sculpture from the British Council collection.*
London: Sothebys. *A positive view.*
Kent: Kent Instistute of Art and Design. *Crossroads.*
New Plymouth: Govett-Brewster Art Gallery. *Power works: from the MCA collection* (essay by Wystan Curnow).
Seoul, Korea: Seoul 600 International Art Festival. *Humanism and technology: the human figure in industrial society.*

1995   Austria: Kunsthalle Krems. *Wasser und Wein: zwie Dinge des Lebens.*

1996   Frankfurt: Frankfurter Kunstverein. *Prospect 96.*
        London: Hayward Gallery and the British Film Institute. *Spellbound: art and film* (essay by
            Michael O'Pray).
        Paris: Centre Georges Pompidou. *La photographie contemporaine.*
        Nice: Centre Municipal de la Photographie. *Septembre de la photo 96. IVe biennale, 'La
            Promendae des Anglais'.*

1997   Auckland: Artspace. *alt.nature.*
        London: Purdy Hicks Gallery. *A cloudburst of material possessions: a fantasy on a drawing by
            Leonardo da Vinci.*
        Ridgefield, Connecticut: The Aldrich Museum of Contemporary Art. *Making it real.*

Articles and reviews

1977   Kelly, Moira. 'David Hockney, Boyd Webb'. *Art Monthly.* no 3, January, pp 25-26.
        Williams, Peter. 'Boyd Webb'. *Studio International.* no 2, pp 154-155.

1978   Davies, Allan. 'In brief'. *Art Monthly.* no 18, pp 28-29.

1979   Castle, Ted. 'Peter Hutchinson & Boyd Webb in New York'. *Art Monthly.* no 27, pp 23-24.

1980   Armstrong, Richard. 'Invented images'. *Artforum.* vol XVIII, no 9, p 88.

1981   Bell, Leonard. 'Photophantasmagoria'. *New Zealand Listener.* 14 November, pp 34-35.
        Fisher, Jean. 'Boyd Webb'. *Art Monthly.* no 45, p 20.
        Lavell, Stephen. 'Boyd Webb'. *Arts Review.* vol 33, pt 9, May, pp 184-185.
        Roberts, John. 'Reviews'. *Artscribe.* no 29, June, p 52 ff.

1982   Blackley, Roger. 'The fourth biennale of Sydney: New Zealanders in Australia'. *Art New
            Zealand.* no 24, Winter, pp 26-31.
        Thiel, H. 'Boyd Webb: Photoskulpturen'. *Kunstforum International.* pt 4, June, p 153.

1983   Patrick, Keith. 'The sculpture show'. *Studio International.* vol 196, no 1003, pp 34-37.
        Van der Kaap, Gerald. 'Boyd Webb'. *Artforum.* vol 22, no 3, November, p 89.

1984   'Boyd Webb.' *The Face.* no 48, April, pp 64-65.
        Beaumont, Mary Rose. 'William Coldstream, Boyd Webb.' *Arts Review.* vol 36, part 13,
        6 July, pp 342-343.
        Morgan, Stuart. 'Boyd Webb'. *Beaux-Arts Magazine.* no 13, May, pp 24-29, 98.
        Morgan, Stuart. 'London – scenes and songs from Boyd Webb'. *Artforum.* vol 23, no 3,
            November, p 113.
        Walker, Ian. 'Boyd Webb'. *Fotografie.* no 35, October/November, pp 109-114.
        Walker, Ian. 'Boyd Webb'. *Creative Camera.* no 238, December, pp 1631-1635.

1985   Boonstra, Rommert. 'Fotograaf Boyd Webb en de Werkelijkheid van de Schijn'.
            Avenue. July.
        Henry, Clare. 'L'indifférent'. *Arts Review XXXVII.* no 4, 1 March, pp 106-107.
        Januszczak, Waldemar. 'L'indifférent'. *Artscribe.* no 51, March, pp 63-65.

Kinmonth, Patrick. 'Neo-logic of Boyd Webb'. *Vogue*. February, p 138.
Paltzer, Rolf. 'Täuschung um der Wahrheit willen'. *Art*. no 11, November, pp 96-102.
Taylor, Brandon. 'L'indifférent'. *Art Monthly*. no 84, March, pp 14-15.

1986 Cooke, Lynne. 'Impresa'. *Flash Art*. no 130, October/November, pp 62-64.
Ellis, Stephen. 'Boyd Webb at Sonnabend'. *Art in America*. January, p 134.
'Die Welt als Vorstellung – Die Vorstellung als Welt'. *Kunstforum International*. no 84, June-August, pp 72-115.
Hjort, O E. 'Britain seen from the north: et blik pa den nye Engelske skulptur'. *Louisiana Revy*. vol 26, pt 2, March, pp 4-7, 51.
Morgan, Stuart. 'Paper moon'. *Parkett*. no 9, June, pp 91-93 (pp 94-97 in German).
Silverthorne, Jeanne. 'Boyd Webb'. *Artforum*. vol XXIV, no 6, February, pp 103-104.
Stefanides, Manos. 'Nominoteta kai lathrokheiria stis plastikes tekhnes'. *Eikastika*. no 58, October, pp 32-33.

1987 Baker, Tom. 'Expo – Boyd Webb'. *The Face*. no 85, pp 95-97.
Gooding, Mel. 'Boyd Webb'. *Flash Art*. no 136, October, p 103.
Higgens, Judith. 'Britain's new "New Generation"'. *ArtNews*. vol 86, no 10, December, pp 118-122.
Morgan, Stuart. 'Boyd Webb at Whitechapel'. *Vogue*. May, p 28.
Pixi, G. 'Boyd Webb'. *Juliet Art Magazine*. no 32, June-September, p 35.
Shaw, Lindsey. 'New Zealand artists in Britain'. *Art New Zealand*. no 44, Spring, pp 82-85, 104.
Stathatos, John. 'Boyd Webb'. *Artscribe*. September/October, pp 71-72.

1988 Bell, Leonard. 'NZI: a commentary'. *Art New Zealand*. no 48, Spring, pp 64-67.
Cartwright, Garth. 'Enzed dead zone'. *New Zealand Listener*. 26 March, pp 52-53.
Hagen, Charles. 'Boyd Webb'. *Artforum*. vol 28, no 4, pp 138-139.
Hughes, Ralph. 'Photography through the looking glass'. *Alba*. no 9, pp 26-30.
Johnstone, Mark. 'Theaters of the mind'. *Artweek*. vol 19, no 21, 28 May, pp 1, 11.
Mellor, David. 'Romances of decay, elegies for the future'. *Aperture*. no 113, Winter, pp 52-67.
Morgan, Stuart. 'Global strategy'. *Noema*. no 16, January-March, pp 36-45.
Reynolds, Patrick. 'Beyond the back-cloth: Boyd Webb at the Whitechapel'. *Art New Zealand*. no 46, Autumn, pp 88-91.

1989 Barak, Ami. 'Boyd Webb: sous le tapis volant'. *Art Press*. no 136, May, pp 28-29.
Bennett, David. 'Art and rubbish: contemporary British colour photography'. *Art & Text*. no 32, Autumn, pp 98-105.
Decter, Joshua. 'Boyd Webb'. *Arts Magazine*. no 4, vol 64, December, p 98.
Flusser, Vilem. 'Boyd Webb: on staging'. *European Photography*. vol 10, pt 2, April-June, pp 38-39.
Graham-Dixon, Andrew. 'Neo, no: still faithful to the old guard'. *ArtNews*. vol 88, no 7, September, pp 122-126.
Graham-Dixon, Andrew. 'Blow up'. *The Independent Magazine*. 7 January, pp 38-41.
Hagen, Charles. 'Boyd Webb'. *Artforum*. no 4, vol 28, December, pp 138-139.
Heartney, Eleanor. 'Boyd Webb'. *ArtNews*. vol 88, no 10, December, p 157.
Martin, Rupert. 'Boyd Webb'. *Flash Art*. no 147, Summer, p 158.
Taylor, Brandon. 'Boyd Webb'. *ArtNews*. vol 88, no 4, April, pp 154-155.

| 1990 | 'Lawrence Weiner, Boyd Webb at the Hirshhorn'. *Flash Art.* vol XXIII, no 155, November/December, p 175. |
| 1992 | Barrie, Lita. 'Los Angeles in review'. *Artspace.* vol 16, no 3, May-June, pp 80-81. |

1990 'Lawrence Weiner, Boyd Webb at the Hirshhorn'. *Flash Art.* vol XXIII, no 155, November/December, p 175.

1992 Barrie, Lita. 'Los Angeles in review'. *Artspace.* vol 16, no 3, May-June, pp 80-81.

1993 Green, Charles. 'A constructed reality: aspects of contemporary photography'. *Art & Text.* no 42, May, pp 107-108.
Podromides, Maxime. 'Visions de la Gitane'. *Photographies Magazine.* no 42, June, pp 34-51.

1994 Cork, Richard. 'Disturbing revelations of genesis'. *The Times.* 11 May.
Durden, Mark. 'Boyd Webb'. *Art Monthly.* no 5, May, pp 176-177.
Feaver, William. 'Life as a plasticene sperm'. *The Observer.* 24 April.
Graham-Dixon, Andrew. 'Small objects of desire'. *The Independent.* 3 May.
Hall, James. 'The art in erotica'. *The Guardian.* 14 January.
Mellor, David Alan. 'The fantastic voyage: new works by Boyd Webb, 1992-94'. *Portfolio Magazine.* no 19, Summer, pp 44-51.

1996 Roegiers, Patrick. 'Septembre de la Photo 96'. *Camera International.* no 42, Autumn (issue dedicated to exhibition in Nice).

Interviews and recordings

1984 'Boyd Webb interviewed by Stuart Morgan'. *Creative Camera.* no 238, December, pp 1636-1637 (in French in *Beaux Art Magazine.* no 13, May, pp 24-29, 89).
'Photographs with a difference'. Boyd Webb interviewed by Liz Finch. *Ritz.* no 91, p 6.

1986 'Boyd Webb interviewet'. Boyd Webb interviewed by Stuart Morgan. *Louisiana Revy.* vol 26, pt 2, March, pp 34-37.

1987 'Critics' forum'. William Feaver, Marilyn Butler, Christopher Cook, and Anthony Thwaite on BBC radio 3, 16 May.

Writing by the artist and pageworks

1978 'The mandatory second opinion'. Steele-Perkins, C. and Messer, W (eds), 1980. *About 70 photographs.* London: Arts Council of Great Britain.

1983 'The lobster'. *Furor.* no 8, pp 45-54.

1987 'Inanimations'. Project for *Artforum.* April, pp 110-113.

1988 'Insert: Boyd Webb'. *Parkett.* no 18, December, pp 123-135.
'Boyd Webb'. *Building design.* 18 March, p 34.

1989 'Unearthing nature: land projects by 4 artists 1969-1980'. *Antic.* (compiled by Christina Barton and Priscilla Pitts). no 5, June, pp 75-96.

1991 'Boyd Webb'. *International photography.* no 1, pp 34-38.

1994 'Boyd Webb'. *Blindspot.* no 4, November, unpaginated.

Works in public collections

Auckland: Auckland Art Gallery
Auckland: Auckland Art Gallery (Chartwell Trust)
Bordeaux: Fonds Régional d'Art Contemporain Aquitaine
Brisbane: Queensland Art Gallery
Bruxelles: The European Parliament
Canberra: National Gallery of Australia
Christchurch: Robert McDougall Art Gallery
Clisson: Fonds Régional d'Art Contemporain Pays de la Loire
Düsseldorf: Kunsthalle
Eindhoven: Stedelijk Van Abbemuseum
Houston: Museum of Fine Arts
La Roche-sur-Yon: Musée de la Roche-sur-Yon
Lisbon: Calouste Gulbenkian Foundation
London: Arts Council of Great Britain
London: Contemporary Arts Society
London: Chase Manhattan Bank
London: British Council
London: Tate Gallery
London: Victoria and Albert Museum
Los Angeles: Museum of Contemporary Art
Leeds: Leeds City Art Gallery
Limoges: Fonds Régional d'Art Contemporain Limousin
Lyon: Fonds Régional d'Art Contemporain Rhône-Alpes
Melbourne: National Gallery of Victoria
Minneapolis: Walker Art Center
Montreal: Musée d'Art Contemporain
Paris: Fonds National d'Art Contemporain
Paris: Musée National d'Art Moderne, Centre Georges Pompidou
Rotterdam: Museum Boymans Van Beuningen
Salford: Salford Museum and Art Gallery
Southampton: Southampton Art Gallery
Sydney: Art Gallery of New South Wales
Sydney: Museum of Contemporary Art
Tenerife: Atlantis Museum
Wellington: Museum of New Zealand Te Papa Tongarewa
Williamstown: Williams College Museum of Art
Zürich: Kunsthalle

Illustrations

This is a chronological list of works illustrated. They are unique colour photographs unless otherwise stated. Dimensions are in centimetres, height before width.

Eels **1971** 12
black and white photograph
29.5 x 37.5

Middle of the road sculpture **1971** 10
black and white photograph
29.1 x 18.8

Herbert Groves **1973** 69
2 photographs + text (edition of 3)
21 x 15 each

Wakatipu **1973** 68
black and white photographs + text
23.8 x 98.5 + 13 x 12 cm mounted
(1997 exhibition version 61.5 x 92.5)

Holothurians **1974** 58
black and white photograph + text
34.5 x 25.5

Script for 'Preview' **1974** 15
black and white photograph + text
40.5 x 32

Altruism and the law of diminishing 16-17
returns **1976**
3 photographs (edition of 3)
21.5 x 27 each

Mrs Barnes **1976** 71
2 photographs (edition of 3)
35 x 29.5 each

The lobster **1976** 70
2 photographs + text (edition of 3)
25.5 x 20 each

Cipher and decipher **1977** 44
2 photographs (edition of 3)
25.7 x 18.5 each

Prehensile torpor **1977** 77
composite photograph (edition of 3)
27 x 43

The microbe as Van Leewenhoek 72-73
may have seen it **1977**
2 photographs
22 x 17.5 each

The conservationist **1978** 78
(edition of 3)
25.5 x 30.5

The mandatory second opinion **1978** 76
(edition of 3)
29 x 37.5

Escapist **1979** 81
39.5 x 47.5

River crossing **1979** 79
28.5 x 35

The light and shade of expedience **1979** 75
(edition of 3)
28 x 35.5 cm

Untitled (pink curtain) **1979** 74
50 x 35

Chapped hands **1980** 80
(edition of 3)
73 x 91

Distressed hose **1980** 49
2 photographs (edition of 3)
28 x 23 each

Guillemots **1981** 166
102 x 75.5

One bird **1981** 19
79 x 101

Eclipse **1982** 32
pastel drawing
25 x 30

Kiss **1982** 83
76 x 102

Index